James Morton is the author of the hugely successful *Gangland* series. He has a great deal of experience as a solicitor specialising in criminal work and was editor-in-chief of *New Law Journal* for many years.

THE HIDDEN
Lives of
LONDON
STREETS

A Walking Guide to Soho,
Holborn and Beyond

JAMES MORTON

ROBINSON

ROBINSON

First published in Great Britain in 2018 by Robinson

Copyright © James Morton, 2018

13 5 7 9 10 8 6 4 2

A CIP catalogue record for this book is available from the British Library

ISBN: 978-1-47213-926-9

Typeset in Scala by TW Type, Cornwall
Printed and bound in Great Britain by CPI Group (UK) Ltd, Croydon CR0 4YY

Papers used by Robinson are from well-managed forests and other
responsible sources

MIX
Paper from
responsible sources
FSC® C104740

Robinson
An imprint of
Little, Brown Book Group
Carmelite House
50 Victoria Embankment
London EC4Y 0DZ

An Hachette UK Company
www.hachette.co.uk

www.littlebrown.co.uk

For Dock Bateson, with love and thanks

Contents

Introduction

In the long-running television programme *Bargain Hunt*, auctioneer Charles Hanson, one of the experts who advises the contestants on whether they should buy a chosen object, often says of a piece of porcelain or glass, 'If only it could speak . . . what a story it could tell.' And the same is true of a street, particularly one in central London, which has had history pass through it, in some cases, for over a thousand years.

Areas have changed dramatically over the years. Some have flourished while others have sunk, only to be revived. Saffron Hill is one, and Covent Garden another. Who, now, would have thought that the first derived its name from the saffron grown there? It became a very unhealthy area until the 1960s when, with a property boom, it began a revival which continues to this day. From the eighteenth century, Covent Garden, along with Seven Dials, was a dangerous slum until after the Second World War, its rejuvenation beginning when the fruit market was relocated. Old Compton Street, once the home of the Italian racecourse gangs, has been transformed into a predominantly gay and welcoming area. Chinatown was only born in the 1960s.

On the streets themselves, many changes have taken place. Tourists may no longer feed the pigeons in Trafalgar Square; gone are the flower sellers who used to sit at the statue of Eros in Piccadilly Circus; no longer can fire-engines from the fire station in Shaftesbury Avenue go round the wrong side of the statue to get to a blaze. The Street Offences Act 1956 cleared the working girls, wearing their hats and gloves, off the pavements in Soho and Coventry Street. And twenty or thirty years ago, there used to be conmen swindling tourists with 'Find the Lady' or the 'Three Card Trick'. Now the police have cleared them off the streets too.

In the 1950s, with the revival of traditional jazz, there used to be a little band called The Happy Wanderers who could be found busking on the pavement edge in Oxford Street and Charing Cross Road playing old Dixieland numbers. Now, buskers themselves have almost vanished from the streets. At the Trafalgar Square end of the Charing Cross Road, there used to be a pavement artist who recreated the Mona Lisa in chalk; in Leicester Square, outside the Empire Cinema, there was an escapologist who was tied in chains and put in a sack. Now, in Oxford Street, there is a man who creates a sand dog. In Covent Garden, there are various street performers a few steps away from the Underground station. Fashions have changed, and buildings along with them.

There is no longer any enthusiasm for the 100-frame billiard and snooker matches of the first half of the twentieth century, when many a happy and idle afternoon could be spent watching the legendary Joe Davis and the Australian Walter Lindrum make endless cannons around the table. So Thurston's Hall in Leicester Square has gone, making way for an addition to Fanum House, the London headquarters of the Automobile Association. At 19 Soho Square, the other great snooker venue, Burroughes Hall, went the same way in 1967 and is now another office block.

Some things are not as they might seem. The Law Courts may look as though they were built centuries ago, and the same applies to Tower Bridge. In fact, the Law Courts are not Gothic architecture but Gothic revival and were built in the late nineteenth century. Similarly, Tower Bridge was opened in 1894, and at one time its high-level, open walkways were a haunt of prostitutes and pickpockets, rather like Burlington Arcade of a century and a half ago.

Over the years, houses have been pulled down and rebuilt, theatres and cinemas have come and gone. For example, the Tivoli at 68 The Strand was first a restaurant and beer garden before becoming a music hall and then a cinema, where the silent *Ben Hur* with Ramon Novarro was first shown and where Samuel Goldwyn premièred the first British talkie, *Bulldog Drummond*, starring Ronald Colman. It eventually closed in 1957 and was demolished and replaced by a department store, which itself was later converted into New South Wales House for the Australian Government. In turn, in the late 1990s, New South Wales House was replaced by an office block. Lyons' Corner Houses, the quintessentially English establishments for tea and cake, have also vanished.

Even if they still stand, many theatres have had their names changed along with their ownership. The Gielgud Theatre in Shaftesbury Avenue when it opened in 1906 was the Hicks Theatre, named after the actor Seymour Hicks, before it became the Globe in 1909 and the Gielgud in 1994.

The inhabitants of London's buildings have also come and gone. Appropriately, the wrestler, painter, actor and sculptor Sam Rabin's 'Past' and 'Future' winged masks remain on the

Daily Telegraph building in Fleet Street. The futuristic *Daily Express* building, designed in 1932, almost next door still stands, but neither now houses the journalists of the pre- and immediate post-war years. The shift of the newspapers from Fleet Street has also meant a change in the clientele of El Vino's just up the road, which from lunch until early evening would be inhabited by journalists who, by 6.00 p.m., had poured out to make way for the barristers who took over. There, until the 1980s, women were prohibited from standing at the bar and men had to wear ties. Times and manners change.

This book, then, is a collection of tales these central London streets would tell if they could talk – about the people who lived and worked in them and of their deaths; of murderers and tricksters, of urban legends, and of events which have led to changes in the law. And for those with the inclination to immerse themselves in up to a thousand years of London's history, many of these walks can be accomplished in an hour, some in even less time.

James Morton, August 2017

CHAPTER ONE

Old and New Compton Streets

The streets were named after Henry Compton who raised funds for a local parish church, eventually dedicated as St Anne's Church in 1686. Running from Wardour Street in the west to the Charing Cross Road as its eastern boundary, Old Compton Street has long been the heart of Soho.

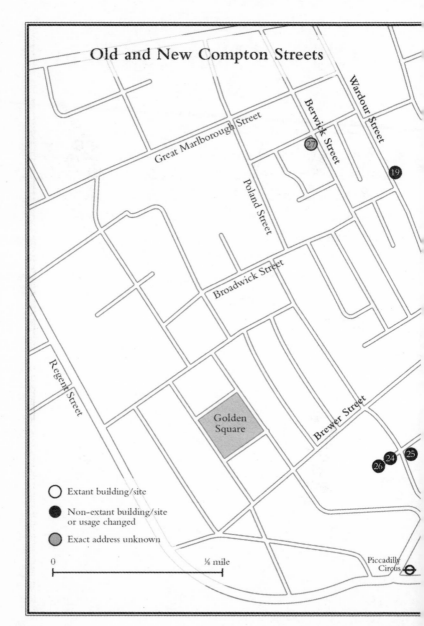

Old and New Compton Streets

Extant building/site

Non-extant building/site
or usage changed

Exact address unknown

0   ⅛ mile

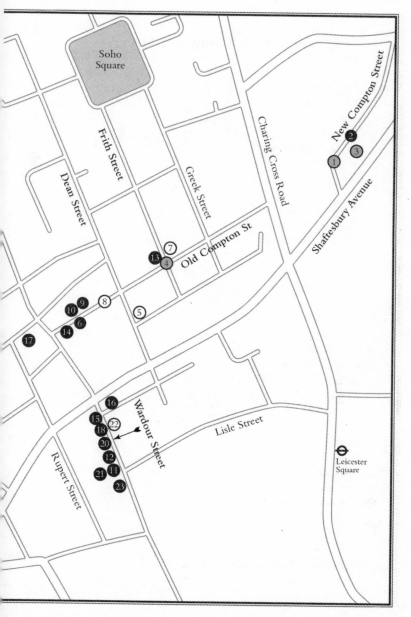

1. OLD AND NEW COMPTON STREETS

1. **Emma Hamilton**, corner of New Compton Street and Stacey Street, Covent Garden.
2. **Fullado Club**, 6 New Compton Street, Covent Garden, WC2H.
3. **Premier Club**, New Compton Street, Soho.
4. **King's Head**, Old Compton Street, Soho.
5. **The York Minster**, 49 Dean Street, Soho, W1D 5BG.
6. **The Black Cat Café and Radio Club**, 55 Old Compton Street, Soho, W1D 6HW.
7. **Fight between Jack Spot and Albert Dimes**, corner of Frith Street and Old Compton Street, Soho.
8. **The Admiral Duncan**, 54 Old Compton Street, Soho, W1D 4UB.
9. **Compton Cinema Club**, 60 Old Compton Street, Soho, W1D 4UG.
10. **Murder of Constance Hinds**, 66 Old Compton Street, Soho, W1D 4UH.
11. **Latin Quarter**, 13-17 Wardour Street, Soho, W1D 6PJ.
12. **Lautrec Bar**, 13-17 Wardour Street, Soho, W1D 6PJ.
13. **Murder of Tony Zomparelli**, 36 Old Compton Street, Soho, W1D 4TT.
14. **2i's Coffee Bar**, 59 Old Compton Street, Soho, W1D 6HR.
15. **Clarkson's Cottage**, 41 Wardour Street, Soho, W1D 6PX.
16. **Shim Sham Club**, 38 Wardour Street, Soho, W1D 6LU.
17. **Isow's**, 8-10 Brewer Street, Soho, W1F 0SD.
18. **Palm Beach Bottles Parties Club**, 37 Wardour Street, Soho, W1D 6PU.
19. **Murder of Evelyn Oatley**, 153 Wardour Street, Soho, W1F 8WG.
20. **Flamingo Club**, 33 Wardour Street, Soho, W1D 6PU.
21. **El Condor**, 17 Wardour Street, Soho, W1D 6PJ.
22. **Leisure Investments amusement arcade**, corner of Gerrard and Wardour Street, Soho.
23. **Log Cabin**, Latin Quarter, Soho.
24. **Jack Solomons' gym**, 41 Great Windmill Street, Soho, W1D 7LU.
25. **Windmill Theatre**, 17-19 Great Windmill Street, Soho, W10 7JZ.
26. **Mac's Dance Hall**, 42 Great Windmill Street, Soho, W1D 7NF.
27. **Jane Goadby's brothel**, corner of Berwick Street and D'Arblay Street, Soho.

Working west, it was in New Compton Street (1) that the fencing master Harry Angelo saw Emma Hamilton, mother of Horatia Nelson, leaning against a post on the corner. That evening he bought her some biscuits and arranged to meet her again. He did not keep the appointment, and the next time he saw her she had graduated to living at Mrs Kelly's brothel in the much more upmarket Arlington Street.

During the Second World War, Elliman Bah, the 6ft 4in son of a Gambian chief, was a favourite of the Colonial Office, who sponsored the Fullado Club (2), a jazz club for black servicemen that Bah owned in New Compton Street. Later, Bah, who at one time owned the very successful greyhound Bob's Choice, rather blotted his copy book by shooting Victor Dimes, the older brother of 'Italian' Albert Dimes, at the Cromwell Club in Nottingham Place. He compounded this bad behaviour by shooting himself in the stomach and was charged with attempted suicide, for which the offence could be charged but not the act of suicide itself. By the time it came to the Old Bailey, things had been sorted out and he received only eighteen months for shooting Dimes. Bah's counsel said he wanted to go back to Gambia as soon as possible and the judge more or less said it was a pity he had ever left.

New Compton Street in the 1960s and 1970s was home to a raft of 'spielers' – for gambling – and drinking clubs including the Premier (3), run by a man called Dave who could always be seen in carpet slippers, and his sister. It was recognised as a place where police, criminals and go-betweens could meet to 'sort things out'. It featured in the inquiry into the conduct of the disgraced West End officer Harold Challenor over whether he had received a bribe in the club. Challenor was supported by the barrister and former police officer William Hemming who held him in high esteem, and Arthur James, who conducted the inquiry, was quite certain that Challenor had not received the bribe. Others were by no means as convinced.

Across Charing Cross Road in Old Compton Street in the nineteenth century the prize-fighter Jem Massey kept the King's Head (4), a noted haunt for patrons of the sport of ratting. Another resident was the dwarfish shoemaker George Wombell who, in around 1800, bought two boa constrictors and started exhibiting them. His collection of exotic animals grew and, by 1810, he was able to found Wombell's Travelling Menagerie which began to tour Britain. By 1830, there were fifteen wagons of animals which comprised, among other species, six lions, a kangaroo, elephants and giraffes. A brass band also travelled with it. He died in 1850 and is buried beneath a statue of his favourite lion, Nero, in Highgate Cemetery.

On 30 September 1843, a German, Peter Keim, was stabbed to death in Marshall Street by a one-time friend, Wilhelm Steltynor, who seems to have tried to castrate him. The inquest jury sitting at the York Minster (5), Dean Street, off Old Compton Street, was told that, when questioned by a constable, Steltynor had said somewhat enigmatically, 'I meant to run it into Mr Keim and had it not been for the leather inside of his trousers, I should have ripped it all out.' He was sentenced to death but the German ambassador intervened and he was reprieved.

In the middle 1920s, the magazine *John Bull* mounted a

campaign against clubs and drinking dens run by foreigners, seeing them as living off English women whom they turned on to the streets. A large number were in Old Compton Street and *John Bull* had some quick success in 1926 by denouncing Francisco Sequi Canals, a Spaniard who, along with his wife Grace, ran the Black Cat Café (6). Canals was deported but not before he had written to the editor complaining of inaccuracies in the article.

There was also the Radio Club at 55 Old Compton Street (6), which *John Bull* thought was 'one room rented at £8 a month where hundreds crowded in to drink after hours and most names given to the police were false'. Next door and along the street were the Movie Club, the Havinoo, the Oak Club and the Premier Club, among others.

On 10 June 1940, after Count Ciano said Mussolini was backing Hitler, the police raided the Italian Club on the Charing Cross Road and took away the waiters. There was a women's march on Old Compton Street and windows were smashed before an Italian woman, Rose Blau, stepped in and pleaded with them, saying that Soho's Italians were mostly British born. Shopkeepers had to put up signs such as 'We are Swiss' and, overnight, the Spaghetti House, which had been running for years, became the British Food Shop.

Around 3.00 p.m. in the afternoon of 11 August 1955, a middle-aged, overweight Jewish man began a knife fight with a rather fitter Italian man on the corner of Frith Street and Old Compton Street (7). The combatants were Jack Comer, the self-styled 'King of the Underworld', known as Jack Spot because, he said, he was 'on the spot' whenever the Jewish community needed him. Others said it was because of a disfiguring mole on his face. The other man was 'Italian' Albert Dimes, the right-hand man of Billy Hill, 'Boss of Britain's Underworld', with whom Spot had once shared control of Soho's rackets and clubs.

The fight was over the control of bookmaking pitches, and they slashed each other to ribbons before it was ended when the wife of a greengrocer into whose shop they had battled hit Spot over the head with a weighing scale. They both staggered out. Spot collapsed in a nearby barber's shop usually frequented by his opponent. Dimes was rushed to hospital by his friends.

Both nearly died, but survived to be charged with affray. After a certain amount of chicanery, including the calling of a bent vicar by Spot to say he was the one who had been attacked, both were acquitted at their subsequent trials at the Old Bailey. However, the fight, which became known as 'The Fight that Never Was', marked the end of the control Spot had over the underworld and led to the rise of the Kray brothers.

At 54 Old Compton Street, the Admiral Duncan (8) was named after Admiral Adam Duncan, who defeated the Dutch fleet at the Battle of Camperdown in 1797. On 22 August 1832, a wooden-legged Irish ex-sailor Dennis Collins who was resident there was charged with high treason for throwing stones at King William IV at Ascot racecourse. Convicted and sentenced to be hanged, drawn and quartered, his sentence was commuted to life imprisonment and he was subsequently transported to Australia.

On 28 December 1881, Justin McCarthy received eight

years' penal servitude for stealing the watch of the then land-lord William Gordon.

In the 1920s, the pub became a hangout for the racecourse gang led by Darby Sabini. In one of the many fights in the pub, a policeman was thrown through a window out on to the street.

By the late 1990s, the Duncan had become a meeting place for the gay and lesbian community, and on the evening of 30 April 1999, neo-Nazi David Copeland nail-bombed the pub, killing three people and wounding around eighty more. Given six life sentences, his minimum tariff was thirty years, although the trial judge spoke of his doubt that it would ever be safe to release him. On 2 March 2007, at a hearing at the High Court, Mr Justice Burton increased Copeland's mini-mum sentence to fifty years, saying this was 'necessary for the protection of the public'. Copeland's release will not occur until 2049 at the earliest, when he will be aged 73.

On 30 October 2004, the Duncan's bar manager David Morley, who had been injured in the bombing, was beaten to death in another homophobic attack, this time near Hungerford Bridge on the South Bank.

It was at 60 Old Compton Street that the Compton Cinema Club (9) pushed the boundaries of the 'blue' film, and in 1977, after a steady diet of unmemorable nude classics such as Harrison Marks' *Naked as Nature Intended*, the manage-ment showed Pasolini's *Salo, or the 120 Days of Sodom*. After the police raided the cinema and threatened the management with keeping a disorderly house, any scene which could possi-bly be construed as obscene was cut before it was shown again.

The cinema later became the Londoner Cinema until, in the 1990s, it became Rainbow Cars, a gay taxi cab company. It is now in use as the kitchen for Balans Soho Society restaurant.

Just down the street, it was on 8 May 1936 that eighteen-year-old Constance Hinds, known as Dutch Leah, was killed at her flat at 66 Old Compton Street (10), beaten to death with a flat iron. No one was ever charged.

One of London's smarter nightclubs in the 1960s was Tolaini's Latin Quarter (11) at the Coventry Street end of Wardour Street. Upstairs was the Lautrec Bar (12) where David Knight was stabbed to death. Tony Zomparelli, the man responsible, immediately left the country and returned to his roots in Italy until he thought things had quietened down. He then returned and was given four years for manslaughter.

After his release, on the afternoon of 4 September 1974, Zomparelli was playing a pinball machine in an amusement arcade in Old Compton Street (13) – appropriately called Wild Life – when he was shot and killed by two masked men. One killer was certainly George Bradshaw, who also went under the alias of Maxie Piggott, and he named Nicky Gerard as his partner. It was said that the contract had been taken out by Ronnie Knight whose brother David had been stabbed to death by Zomparelli. Knight and Gerard were both acquitted but later Knight admitted he had been the contractor. Subsequently, he retracted the admission.

In June 1982, Nicky Gerard was shot and killed when he left his daughter's birthday party in south-east London. His cousin, Tommy Hole, was acquitted of his murder. Seventeen years later, Hole was killed in an east London public house.

On the other side of the street, the Australian wrestlers Paul Lincoln, who appeared as 'Dr Death', and Ray Hunter opened their 2i's Coffee Bar (14). It became the home of skiffle and a launching pad for performers such as Tommy Steele. Once a target of protection racketeers who attacked and slashed the doorman, the threat evaporated when they returned only to find the gigantic Hunter now on the door.

At right angles to Old Compton Street and separating it from Brewer Street is Wardour Street. Originally Wellington Street, in the late seventeenth century the street was named after Sir Edward Wardour who had land in the area.

The diminutive and eccentric theatrical wig maker and costumier William Berry 'Willy' Clarkson, who used to wash his own socks and recycle letters sent to him, had rooms opposite a notorious public lavatory, known locally as 'Clarkson's Cottage', in Dansey Place off Wardour Street. The urinal had featured in the 1913 case of Holton v. Mead, a landmark case concerning gay soliciting. Evidence was presented and purported to show that the carrying of a powder puff by a young Welsh visitor to London could be used to establish his homosexual tendencies and so indicate his intention to solicit. When the lavatory was closed after the Second World War, it was allegedly bought by a wealthy New Yorker and installed in his garden.

For nearly fifty years, most theatre programmes in London carried the legend 'Wigs by Clarkson', but unfortunately he had two other undesirable professions – blackmailer and insurance fraudster – to go with his legitimate one. In all, eleven of his business premises burned down.

There were unproven allegations that, in October 1934, Clarkson had been murdered, but subsequently the dishonest solicitor's clerk William Hobbs and the talented but alcoholic solicitor Edmond O'Connor were convicted of forging his will. They received five and seven years respectively.

A London County Council blue plaque unveiled in 1966 commemorates Clarkson at 41–43 Wardour Street (15). The foundation stone of his Wardour Street premises had been laid by the actress Sarah Bernhardt, and the coping stone by actor Henry Irving.

Between the wars, the Shim Sham Club at number 38 (16), named after a tap dance routine, was opened by Jack Isow and the singer Ike Hatch. According to police records, it was frequented by prostitutes, thieves, ponces and lesbians. At the time, Isow himself was described as an 'alien with a very nasty record'. He also ran the Majestic Billiard Hall below the Shim Sham. He fell foul of the Sabinis and, in May 1933, two of their henchmen, Tommy Mack and Sidney Buonocore, tried to destroy the club.

But like so many, as the years went by, Isow became respectable and his restaurant, Isow's, at 8–10 Brewer Street (17), was a fashionable place to dine in the 1950s and 1960s. In the basement was the Jack of Clubs nightclub. It was there that the boxer Nosher Powell, then running the door, refused the Kray Twins entry because they were not wearing ties. Charlie Kray was sent by them to see Powell and the matter was patched over, but Powell said that for some time he took care to walk down the centre of the road when he had locked up the premises.

With many Italians interned during the Second World

War, others moved into the protection of their clubs and, on 30 April 1941, Antonio 'Babe' Mancini stabbed the pimp Hubby Distleman to death at the Palm Beach Bottles Parties Club at 37 Wardour Street (18). Coincidentally, the club was where the Maltese vice king Eugenio Messina had met Marthe Watts, his long-time mistress and controller of the girls who worked for him. Mancini, the doorman of the premises, claimed he had walked into an upstairs club where fighting had already broken out between Albert Dimes and a Jewish contingent. He had found a dagger on the floor and used it to defend himself. After a series of appeals which went to the House of Lords to decide what amount of provocation was needed to reduce a murder charge to manslaughter, Mancini was hanged.

The prostitute and ex-actress Evelyn Oatley, also known as Nita Ward, was killed in her flat at 153 Wardour Street (19) on 10 February 1942. Her throat had been cut and her genitals mutilated with a tin opener. Her death was the last in a series of killings in and around the West End by Gordon Cummings. He was ultimately caught because he had dropped his gas mask when he tried to strangle another young woman he had picked up at the Trocadero on the corner of Piccadilly Circus.

In October 1962, the musician and small-time dope dealer Aloysius 'Lucky' Gordon fought with another dealer Johnny Edgecombe in the Flamingo Club at number 33 (20), over the favours of call-girl Christine Keeler. Gordon was slashed with a knife and needed seventeen stitches. The story goes that when they were removed, he sent them to Edgecombe.

Three years later, in the early hours of 15 September 1965,

Lionel William 'Curly' King, who ran a protection gang in Soho, was stabbed in the backside outside the Flamingo and staggered into the American Pizza café for help. The year before, King had been given an *ex gratia* payment and a free pardon after he claimed to have had evidence planted on him by Detective Sergeant Harold Challoner in 1963. It is thought his stabbing was part of an effort by the Kray Twins to take over protection of the Flamingo.

Clubs changed names as often as men their underwear. Diana Dors' boyfriend, the bodybuilder Tommy Yeardsley, ran the El Condor at number 17 (21) before it was taken over by property racketeer Peter Rachman in the 1960s and re-launched as La Discotheque, with 'Bohemian décor'. On the opening night, Rachman was photographed accompanied by his dark-haired girlfriend Mandy Rice-Davies, with his foot on a toilet seat signed 'Peter'. Stories have it that Mandy was cleaning a glass for Rachman at the bar when Ronnie Kray shouted over for a drink. Mandy told him that she was not a barmaid but Kray insisted, gripping her wrist. She slapped him and called over Rachman's minder, Jimmy Houlihan. Seeing who it was, Houlihan went to fetch Rachman, who pleaded with Mandy to apologise. The story goes that he paid £5,000 in settlement of the argument.

Rachman had good security on the door of La Discotheque in the form of British heavyweight champion Bert Assirati and the fearsome 'Mad' Fred Rondel, who had his own club in Rupert Street and who had once bitten a man's ear off. But guns tend to do more damage than fists and teeth. In March 1963, the relief doorman, ex-Guardsman Dennis John Raine, was shot in the leg. He had refused entry to two men earlier in the evening.

Yury Gomez, who almost burned to death on 3 April 1989 at the Leisure Investments amusement arcade which stood on the corner of Gerrard and Wardour Streets (22), survived to name the killer Victor Castigador, a Filipino who worked as a security guard in the arcade. When the police arrived they found two other security guards dead as well as 26-year-old cashier Debbie Alvarez, who was still alive. All four had been bound, doused with a flammable liquid, set alight and locked in the safe, which had been emptied of its contents.

Two days later, the police arrested Castigador at a flat in Bow. He had £480 of the stolen £8,685 in his possession. Castigador, who claimed he had been an assassin for the Filipino Government, had set up the robbery because others had been promoted ahead of him and he had not been given a bonus. At one time he had worked at the company's Oxford Street arcade where he had broken the jaw of a client he thought to be troublesome. He was sentenced to life imprisonment with a recommendation that he serve a minimum of twenty-five years.

At the south end of Wardour Street was the Log Cabin (23), a basement drinking club which held around thirty people. The East End hard man, the late Mickey Bailey, recalled:

'Out of them thirty there'd be thieves of all descriptions – robbers, key men, hoisters, safeblowers, jump-up men. One might be southside and he'd say, "How you going, anything about?"

'"Yeah, I don't know if you'd be interested . . ."

'You didn't go down looking for a job as if you was going to the labour exchange but you might be down there and someone would say, "You're the very man I want to see." It was a neutral place and a very convenient place for thieves to meet. There was a fellow on the door – Dummy. There was very few arguments but if you wanted someone got out, Dummy would do it for you.'

Brewer Street, named because of the number of breweries there, was the home of duellist and French spy the Chevalier d'Eon, who spent forty-nine years of his life as a man and thirty-four as a woman, giving rise to the English word 'eonism', a synonym for transvestism.

In 1763, d'Eon held the office of chargé d'affaires at the French Embassy, and found himself quarrelling with the French Ambassador. Some time later, d'Eon was invited to the Embassy in Soho Square where the Ambassador gave him some drugged wine. D'Eon managed to make his excuses and refused the help of two sedan carriers who had been engaged to take him to the river and drown him.

Shortly after that, he barricaded himself in his Brewer Street home guarded by men from his old regiment until the threats against him were withdrawn. In 1771, there was intense speculation over whether the Chevalier was indeed a man or a woman with the *Morning Post* offering odds of 4/7 on his being a man with wagers totalling £20,000.

He died on 22 May 1819 aged about eight-five at the Millman Street Foundling hospital where he had been living for some years. The next day, his body was dissected in the presence of the Earl of Yarmouth and T. Copeland, a Surgeon of Golden Square, who certified, '[I] have found the male organs in every respect perfectly formed.'

One of the hot spots in the 1950s was Dilly's Café in Brewer Street and the troubles there came on the last weekend of the month and the first of the next when the American soldiers were paid. After two weeks, they ran out of money and there was relative peace and quiet until the next pay day. One man wrote to his MP saying that his wife was afraid to go out at night but his complaint was dismissed as an exaggeration.

Running off Shaftesbury Avenue near to Piccadilly Circus, the boxing promoter Jack Solomons' gym was in Great Windmill Street (24). Almost opposite was the Windmill Theatre (25) which staged non-stop revues in which girls posed naked except for a few strategically placed stars. Originally it had been a cinema – the Palais de Luxe – and was then taken over in 1932 by Vivian Van Damm who also promoted speedway racing before the Second World War. It opened at noon every weekday and was so popular that soon there were half a dozen or more rivals. But the Windmill was the one that lasted, billing itself as 'We Never Closed', which made it unique during the Blitz. In the week of 7 September 1940, there were forty-two shows running in theatres in the West End, and the following week there was only the revue at the Windmill. Wags said it should really have been 'We Never Clothed', and the revue became very popular with servicemen on leave.

In those days, most unmarried and some married men had never seen a semi-naked woman. Over the years, the cream of

British comedians, including Bruce Forsyth, Tony Hancock, Peter Sellers and Tommy Cooper, appeared there in front of an audience just waiting for them to finish their routines. At the end of each show, the men known as 'jimmers' climbed over the seats to get a better position for the next one.

On 4 September 1945, American serviceman Private Thomas Edward Croft stabbed a waiter, Gordon Johnson, to death in a row over a girl called Lena at Mac's Dance Hall, 42 Great Windmill Street (26). Also known as Rita, she was one of what was known at the time as the 'Piccadilly Commandos', semi-professional prostitutes who frequented Soho at the end of the war. Engaged to Johnson, she was also sleeping on a commercial basis with Croft's friend Joe Devine. When Croft and Devine found Johnson dancing with the girl, a fight broke out. Croft produced a dagger from his boot and killed Johnson. He was sentenced to life imprisonment by an American court martial.

At right angles to Brewer Street, Berwick Street was where the madam Jane Goadby introduced the luxurious French-style brothel to London in around 1750 (27). After a visit to Paris, she opened a house where the girls were decked out in lace and silk and underwent a weekly medical examination. Goadby had a long run as a madam. In 1779, the *Nocturnal Revels* commented that she was still 'laying in good stocks of clean goods, warranted proof for the races and watering places during the coming summer'.

One of the girls in her house, Elizabeth Armistead, married the Whig leader Charles James Fox at the age of 45. She lived to be 91, and among her earlier patrons had been the Prince of

Wales, later George IV. Today, Berwick Street is the subject of major rebuilding but is still home to one of the oldest London street markets.

CHAPTER TWO

Gerrard and Lisle Streets

The first houses in Gerrard Street – numbers 15 and 16 – were built in the late 1670s and the larger houses which followed were later occupied by literary and artistic figures such as Dr Samuel Johnson.

During the anti-Catholic Gordon Riots, the magistrates used the Turk's Head at number 9 to try some of the rioters. In happier times, it was the home of The Club, founded by the painter Sir Joshua Reynolds, whose members included Johnson, as well as his biographer James Boswell.

At number 27, the Hotel de Boulogne was the home of the French government-in-exile during the Second World War.

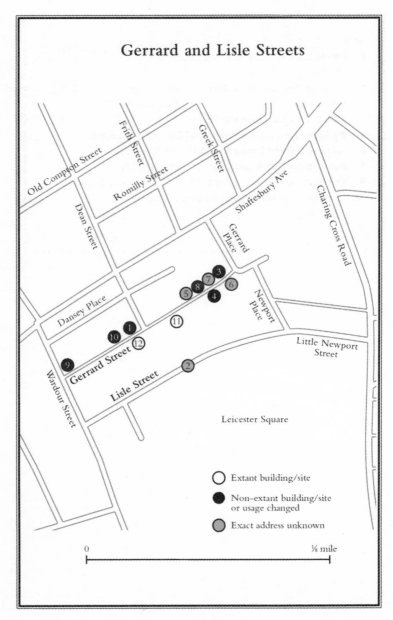

Gerrard and Lisle Streets

Old Compton Street

Frith Street

Greek Street

Romilly Street

Shaftesbury Ave

Charing Cross Road

Dean Street

Gerrard Place

Dansey Place

Newport Place

Little Newport Street

Wardour Street

Gerrard Street

Lisle Street

Leicester Square

○ Extant building/site

● Non-extant building/site or usage changed

● Exact address unknown

0   ⅛ mile

2. GERRARD AND LISLE STREETS

1. **Pelican Club**, 34-35 Gerrard Street, Soho, W1D 6JA.
2. **The Philary**, Lisle Street, Soho.
3. **Studio of George Harrison Marks**, 4 Gerrard Street, Soho, W1D 5PE.
4. **The 43 Club**, 43 Gerrard Street, Soho, W1D 5QG.
5. **Palm Court Club**, Gerrard Street, Soho.
6. **Big Apple**, a few doors down from 43 Gerrard Street, Soho.
7. **Coloured Colonial Service Club**, 5 Gerrard Street, Soho.
8. **New Cabinet Club**, 6 Gerrard Street, Soho, W1D 5PG.
9. **Kaleidoscope**, corner of Gerrard Street and Wardour Street, Soho.
10. **Bonsoir/Hide-a-Way**, 16 Gerrard Street, Soho, W1D 6JE.
11. **Loon Fung**, 39 Gerrard Street, Soho, W1D 5QD.
12. **BRB bar**, 32 Gerrard Street, Soho, W1D 6JA.

Gerrard and Lisle Streets were not always part of London's Chinatown. On 15 November 1712, Charles 3rd Baron Mohun fought a duel with the Duke of Hamilton over a contested legacy and both died from their wounds. When Mohun's body was brought to his house in Gerrard Street, it is said that his wife was less than pleased after his body was flung on the best bed. Mohun and Hamilton had suffered such horrific injuries that the Government tried to pass legislation banning duels.

In 1694, Mohun had been luckily acquitted of murder in a trial at the House of Lords when he and his friend Captain Richard Hill stabbed a William Montford in the mistaken belief that he was Hill's rival for the affections of the actress Mrs Bracegirdle. Mohun then went on to kill another man – coincidentally another Captain Hill – and before his duel with Hamilton at the age of twenty he had been acquitted of aiding and abetting the Earl of Warwick when he killed Captain Richard Coote.

The home of the prize-fight in London became the celebrated Pelican Club (1) which opened its doors in Wardour Street in 1887, before moving to Gerrard Street. This was the post-bare-knuckle fighting era, when skin gloves were introduced. The Pelican took its name from a stuffed bird which was kept proudly on display, along with a stuffed flamingo. Generally, the wealth and rank of its members kept the fights safe from the prying eyes of the police, and one intruding officer was told by Sir Robert Peel, 'My father did not invent you to interfere with me.' Large bets were placed, and one of the club's protégés was Jem Smith, the All-England Heavyweight

Champion, who fought a 106-round draw with Jake Kilrann. Shortly after that, he was matched on the club premises in a gloved bout with a black American, Peter Jackson. Smith was being badly beaten when he was disqualified for trying to push Jackson out of the ring to save his masters' wagers.

The club's other functions were for members' gambling and drinking. And an unwritten rule was that the bar stayed open as long as anyone had any money left. Another specialist skill of the members was dodging their creditors. On one occasion, Captain Fred Russell, a member whose debts were considerable, arranged (under an assumed name) to be hired by one of his creditors. He then chased himself around England – all expenses paid – before reporting that the Captain had gone abroad.

In 1890, residents of Gerrard Street complained of cabs coming and going late into the night and rowdyism at the club. A long rearguard action followed in which the club's lawyers argued that Gerrard Street had always been a 'late' street, home to many after-hours clubs, and that perhaps the noise was coming from the Italian Cooks' and Waiters' Club next door, and, in any event, the music was no louder than a Salvation Army band. It took until December before Mr Justice Rohmer granted the neighbours a partial victory ruling that no cabs could be hailed between midnight and 7.00 a.m. *The Times* thought that the decision 'robs the weary Bohemians of their cabs during the very hours in which they are accustomed to seek their beds'.

In contrast to the Pelican, the National Sporting Club was founded at 43 King Street, Covent Garden in March 1891, attracting around 1,300 members in its heyday. Bouts were fought after dinner and talking was banned during rounds. In 1909, the club introduced the Lonsdale Belt, awarded to the British champion at each weight. It later moved to the Stadium Club, Holborn, and later to Soho Square, and then to the Hotel Splendide in Piccadilly.

In January 1933, a one-time West End actor, the lank-haired Harry Raymond, received five years for blackmail. In his pomp he had appeared in the West End in the stage version of Edgar Wallace's racing thriller *The Calendar*, but those days were long gone. On his release on licence in October 1936, he took the lease of the Philary (2), a café in Lisle Street, from where he led what was described the next year at the Old Bailey as a twelve-strong 'gang of blackmailers and sodomites'. Additionally, up to forty young men were groomed and kitted out by Raymond before being placed in hotels, restaurants and cinemas to solicit wealthy-looking men. Part of the training was in patience, and it was only after a series of theatre visits and late-night suppers that there was the obligatory visit to the hotel room or flat. And there the young male blackmailer, now in tears, would say he would be obliged to tell his parents or, worse, his brother, who just happened to be outside.

The gang included one man who, posing as the vicar of an East End parish, sought out the errant serving military men and other gentlemen, suggesting they might like to pay £500 for the expenses of the defiled youth to go to Australia. In just over a year, one senior officer paid £10,000 for his indiscretions to Raymond whose web spread from Cornwall to the Shetlands. Apart from his team of blackmailers, Raymond was also running foreign prostitutes from the café. On this occasion, he received ten years.

Number 4 Gerrard Street (3) was the studio of George Harrison Marks, one of the pioneers of the British sex film industry, making such notable films as *Naked as Nature Intended*, which starred his partner, the model Pamela Green, who founded Kamera Productions with him. Marks ended his career in 1992 with *Spanker's Paradise, Parts I & II*.

By no means a conventional Irish beauty, the sad-eyed, drab and dowdy Ma Meyrick is said to have run her flagship, the 43 Club (4) in Gerrard Street (where centuries earlier John Dryden had lived), with a rod of iron. An astute businesswoman, even if she had not taken up her career until her forties, she educated her children with the profits. One son went to Harrow, the daughters to Roedean. She would expel Darby Sabini's men, Billy Kimber's Elephant Boys and rowdy Oxbridge undergraduates with the same aplomb. The police officer Robert Fabian recalled her saying, 'Fun is fun, but vulgarity is vulgarity. Out you go, my boy.'

She certainly did not want any more police attention than was absolutely necessary, so it was to her considerable annoyance that when Brilliant Chang sold his restaurant, he became a partner in the Palm Court Club (5) in Gerrard Street. Chang served a fourteen-month sentence in 1923 for drug dealing and was deported two years later. During his time in England, it is estimated he made several million from drug trafficking, most of which he had sent back to his native China.

Ma Meyrick's downfall came along with that of the police officer George Goddard in 1929. She had been bribing Goddard

to tip her off about impending police raids. He received eighteen months with hard labour and she fifteen months. It did
not stop her operating louche clubs. On her release in May 1932,
she was fined after a police raid. The police evidence included
hearing 'a disgusting song' which had been applauded, and
the solicitation by a prostitute, 'Are you on your own, dear?'
She died in the influenza pandemic of 1933.

A few doors along from the 43 was a 'black' club called
the Big Apple (6). Next door to that was Hell, run by Geoffrey
Dayell and patronised by Sam Henry, who made his fortune
from the bottle party, the invention of Eustace Hoey who ran a
wine merchant's in Warwick Street and Rupert Street. It was
a device to get around the licensing laws and caused no end of
trouble to the police and operators alike. Hoey had come up
with the idea that a client who ordered a drink during licensing hours from the wine shop could have it delivered to the
table of the club he was in. Hoey retired a rich man, before a
change in the licensing laws put an end to the trick.

At the end of the Second World War, there was considerable
trouble between black and white American troops. They had
what amounted to their own clubs but that did not prevent
trouble breaking out. On 17 August 1945, there was extensive
fighting outside the Coloured Colonial Service Club (7) in
Gerrard Street when black and white American servicemen
clashed. When the white soldiers found they were outnum-
bered, they went to the Rainbow Club to collect reinforcements.

In 1950, the gangleader Billy Hill leased the New Cabinet
Club (8) in Gerrard Street from Eva Holder, who that year
was convicted of defrauding Peter Haig Thomas, a former

Cambridge rowing coach. Once married into the aristocracy, at the age of 68 Thomas fell in love with this temptress some thirty years his junior, handing over £35,000. He met her while she had been soliciting in Soho and paid her £2 10s, along with 5s for the maid. From then on it appears to have been love on his part and, in an effort to keep her off the streets, over a period of a year he parted with increasing amounts of cash on the basis that she was investing it in property in Soho or speculating in clubs. He set her up in a flat in Lisle Street and intended to take her with him to Kenya but, because of her convictions for soliciting dating back to December 1929, this was impossible.

Curiously, despite numerous convictions for soliciting, she had none for dishonesty and none for soliciting after he met her. She claimed the money was, in fact, a series of gifts and that he had gone to the police simply because she could not put up with him any more; but the jury and certainly the judge, finding it unbelievable that anyone would part with this sort of money, found against her. She received two years' imprisonment for conspiring to cheat Thomas.

Until the late 1950s, there was no great Chinese presence in Soho. It was still a question of always finding a smile in Lisle Street as the prostitutes paraded there in an essentially Italian *quartier*. It is an East Ender, Francis McGovern, who spoke some Cantonese, who is generally credited with giving the Chinese gamblers their start in the area. The story is that he won the Kaleidoscope (9), a café on the corner of Gerrard and Wardour Streets, in a poker game and allowed the Chinese to use the basement for gambling.

For a time, the new arrivals were prey to home-grown talent. On 16 May 1963, an Irishman received four years at the Old Bailey. He had been running a six-strong but short-lived protection racket demanding money from Chinese gambling dens in Gerrard Street and robbing waiters. In one case, he had used a seventeen-year-old Irish girl to lure waiters into the back of a van.

There were still traditionally run nightclubs in the streets and, in 1965, a case saw the beginning of the gradual erosion of the Kray Twins' empire. The Bonsoir (10) in Gerrard Street, once owned by Albert Dimes and 'Mad' Frank Fraser, became the Hide-a-Way owned by the gay Scottish baronet Hew McCowen. When the Krays demanded a share, he went to the police. Two trials later, it was disclosed that he had convictions for sex offences and had been in mental institutions. The Krays were acquitted and immediately took over the club, renaming it the El Morocco.

If there was any doubt that there were serious crime figures in Soho's Chinese community, Triads or not, it was swiftly dispelled in February 1976. It was then that Kay Wong, a restaurant owner from Basildon, was kicked to death in an illegal gambling club in a basement in Gerrard Street as he sat playing Mah Jong. He suffered fourteen broken ribs as well as a ruptured spleen. The kicks were so savage that the toe of one of the attackers' shoes had split and, later, the police were able to trace a shop in Leeds where a new pair of shoes had been bought and eventually to match that purchase to the shoes used in the murder.

The attackers had wanted to know the address of Wong's

son, Wong Pun Hai, whom they believed to be a member of the 14K Triad group and partly responsible for the murder in December 1975 of one of their relations in Holland. In a subsequent trial, Wong Pun was acquitted. That murder had happened because a dealer, Li Kwok Pun, had failed to make a heroin delivery and the 14K had displayed its displeasure by putting eight bullets into the man's chest.

In March 1982, a knife battle – which left one dead – was fought out in the Loon Fung restaurant (11) at 39 Gerrard Street between the Singapore Boys and the Hong Kong Boys. It seems to have been over a perceived insult at a christening party when a man refused to drink half a glass of brandy. In July that year, seven people died when a petrol bomb was thrown into the basement of the premises.

In 1985, when Sheffield businessman Chan Wai Chau went to a traditional Chinese wedding in Gerrard Street, all went well until seven men arrived together. One walked up to Chan and kicked him, thus identifying him as the target for the others. Three then stood guard while Chan was badly beaten and hit with meat cleavers. No one tried to intervene nor, indeed, could anyone remember afterwards having seen anything at all. For a time it was thought Chan would die and he told the police that both he and the other men were members of the Wo Sing Wo, and had been involved in a quarrel over the rights to the lucrative Hong Kong soap-opera video market.

By the time the case came up for its hearing in 1987, Chan, who had had one of his legs and a thumb amputated, could remember nothing. Neither could he make any identification of his attackers. Nevertheless, they were, perhaps surprisingly, convicted and received, just as surprisingly, modest sentences. By 1991, all but one were back on the streets of their home towns.

The year after Chan's case, another Chinese businessman involved in the video industry was attacked with cleavers in Shaftesbury Avenue. He had earlier brought a lawsuit against a man he had alleged was pirating his videos.

On 3 June 2003, Chinese-born You Yi He, thought to be a member of the 14K, was shot and killed in the BRB bar (12) in Gerrard Street. The gunman, wearing a red shirt and said to be of Chinese appearance with long hair, shot him from a distance of between ten and fifteen feet and then simply walked out of the bar. Various theories were proposed about the murder. One was that it was part of a battle for the control of a human trafficking empire. It was generally believed Snakeheads were behind the killing. The second theory was that it was over unpaid gambling debts owed by You Yi He or, more likely, it was he who was owed money he had been illegally lending to gamblers in a casino in Leicester Square favoured by South-East Asian groups. His death had eliminated the necessity to repay the loan. One thing is clear, however: it was the first time a gun had been used successfully in a Chinese killing in Soho.

CHAPTER THREE

Oxford Street to Piccadilly

Oxford Street was the old road linking London to Oxford and, in the sixteenth century, Piccadilly was known as the Road to Reading. At one time called Portugal Street after Catherine of Braganza, wife of Charles II, the name was changed to Piccadilly after the broad lace collar designed by the landowner Robert Baker, who had made his fortune from making and selling them and who, at one time, had a house there called Piccadilly Hall.

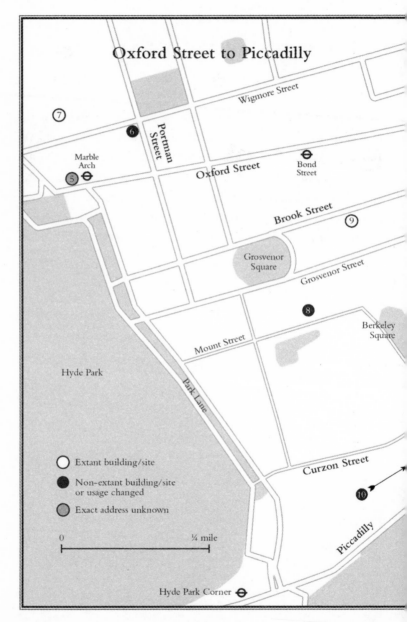

Oxford Street to Piccadilly

Wigmore Street

⑦

❻ Portman Street

Marble Arch

❺ ⊖

Oxford Street

⊖ Bond Street

Brook Street

⑨

Grosvenor Square

Grosvenor Street

❽

Berkeley Square

Mount Street

Hyde Park

Park Lane

Curzon Street

❿

○ Extant building/site

● Non-extant building/site or usage changed

◐ Exact address unknown

0 ¼ mile

Piccadilly

Hyde Park Corner ⊖

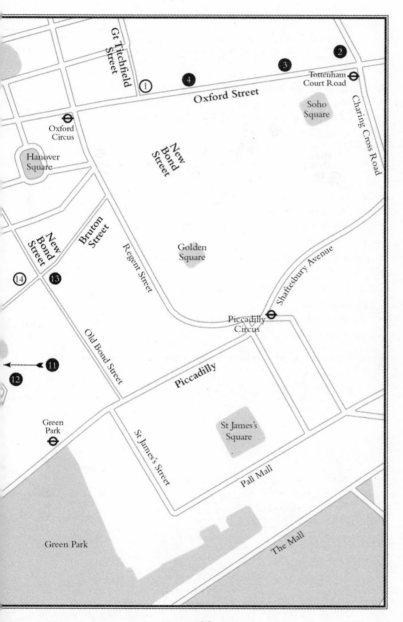

3. OXFORD STREET TO PICCADILLY

1. **Thomas de Quincey's meeting point with Anne**, corner Great Titchfield Street and Oxford Street, Fitzrovia.
2. **Lyons' Corner House**, corner Oxford Street and Tottenham Court Road, Marylebone.
3. **'Dr' Talbot Bridgewater's surgery**, 57 Oxford Street, Marylebone, W1D 1BH.
4. **Wimpy Bar**, Oxford Street, Marylebone.
5. **Tyburn gallows**, corner of Edgware Road, Oxford Street and Marble Arch, Marylebone.
6. **Spencer's Hotel**, Portman Street, Marylebone.
7. **Cumberland Hotel**, Great Cumberland Place, Marylebone.
8. **The Bridge Club**, Mount Street, Mayfair.
9. **Claridge's**, Brook Street, Mayfair.
10. **Arrest of Lola Montez**, Half Moon Street, Mayfair (now the Hilton Hotel).
11. **The Colony Club**, Berkeley Square, Mayfair.
12. **Astor Club**, Lansdowne Row, Mayfair.
13. **London Arts Gallery**, New Bond Street, Mayfair.
14. **Lefevre Gallery**, 31 Bruton Street, Mayfair, W1J 6QS.

It was on the corner of Great Titchfield Street and Oxford Street
(1) in the early years of the nineteenth century that the writer
Thomas de Quincey arranged to meet a fifteen-year-old prostitute, Anne, who had cared for him after he had collapsed from
hunger. He told her he was going to Bristol to borrow money
and would be back in a week's time, after which she should
go to the corner at 6.00 p.m. every evening. He returned regularly at the appointed hour, but she never appeared and he
never found her again.

Lyons' Corner House (2) on the corner of Oxford Street and
Tottenham Court Road was where the Trasart family met for a
family reunion on 20 April 1945. During the meal, 27-year-old
Jack Trasart, who suffered from depression, pulled out a gun
and shot dead his sister Clare and his father and badly injured
his brother. He then turned the gun on himself and, when
it failed to fire, threw it into the bowl of a hanging light. His
explanation was that he had been thinking of killing them for
some years. His sister was an epileptic, his brother had a form
of paralysis in his hands and, as for his father, 'he was miserly,
terribly bigoted and the worst person to have as a father'. He
was found unfit to plead and committed to Broadmoor where
he died soon afterwards.

Back in 1905, the self-styled Australian 'Dr' Talbot
Bridgewater of the Progressive Medical Alliance not only carried on his surgical operations – mainly abortions – from 57
Oxford Street (3), but helping him were a motley crew of criminals including William Shaknell and Lionel Peyton Holmes,
as well as the attractively named Willy 'Moocher' Wigram,
convicted of stealing £1,500 from a Glasgow bank.

Bridgewater certainly looked after his 'friends' – he paid for Moocher's defence. When not at the operating table, Bridgewater's assistants were out on the streets stealing letters and forging cheques – 'scratching' as it was called. Early that year, Bridgewater gave evidence on behalf of Holmes, saying the charge of tendering a forged cheque was a disgrace. The jury twice failed to agree but Bridgewater might have been advised not to enter the witness box. He, Holmes and Shaknell were on trial for theft and forgery at the Old Bailey by the following November, in which the principal prosecution witness was an old convict Charles Fisher, seeking to reduce a ten-year sentence for warehouse breaking by informing on his former friends. After an eleven-day trial, Bridgewater received seven years' penal servitude, Shaknell two years less, and Holmes a modest fifteen months with hard labour.

The dentist Hawley Harvey Crippen, later convicted of the murder of his wife Belle Elmore, was a partner at the Yale Tooth Specialist Company, which had offices at the same address.

On 26 October 1981, a bomb planted by the IRA in a Wimpy Bar (4) on Oxford Street killed explosives expert Kenneth Howorth, the Metropolitan Police officer who was attempting to defuse it. In 1985, IRA volunteers Paul Kavanagh and Thomas Quigley, both from Belfast, were convicted of his murder (along with other attacks including the Chelsea Barracks nail bomb in September 1981) and each received five life sentences with a minimum tariff of thirty-five years. They were released in 1999 under the terms of the Good Friday Agreement.

There is some dispute over exactly where the Tyburn gallows (5) stood at the western end of Oxford Street. Suggestions include west of the junction of Oxford Street and the Edgware Road; 49 Connaught Square; the north side of Bryanston Square; a corner of Upper Seymour Street and the junction of Oxford Street; and the Bayswater Road. It is possible that, at one time or another, the gallows stood at all these places because it was something of a moveable feast. There is, however, a plaque marking the site of Tyburn on a traffic island at the junctions of Edgware Road, Marble Arch and Oxford Street.

In 1782, the body of John Haynes, a professional thief and housebreaker, was taken for dissection to Sir William Blizard, who, as a mark of decency, received the bodies of executed criminals at the Royal College of Surgeons in his formal court dress as president of the college. Apparently, the body showed signs of life, and Sir William managed to revive Haynes. Anxious to know the sensations which the man had experienced at the moment of his hanging, the surgeon questioned him. The only answer he could get was, 'The last thing I recollect was going up Holborn Hill in a cart. I thought then that I was in a beautiful green field; and that is all I remember 'til I found myself in your honour's dissecting room.' History does not seem to have recorded whether he was sent back for a second attempt.

On 7 November the following year, the last man to be hanged at Tyburn was the highwayman John Austin convicted of the murder of a John Spicer. His last words were said to have been: 'Good people, I request your prayers for the salvation of my departing soul. Let my example teach you to shun the bad ways I have followed. Keep good company, and mind the word of God. Lord have mercy on me. Jesus look down with pity on me. Christ have mercy on my poor soul!'

His pious words did Austin no good. Unfortunately, the noose slipped and it took ten minutes for him to choke to death.

The move of the gallows to Newgate did not appeal to everyone, including Dr Samuel Johnson, who remarked, 'The age is running mad over innovations. All the business of the world is to be done in a new way. Men are to be hanged in a new way.'

It was at Spencer's Hotel (6) in Portman Street on 14 March 1922 that the eighteen-year-old pantry-boy Henry Jacoby beat one of the guests, Lady White, to death with a hammer left by a workman in the basement. He had been disturbed by her while stealing from her room. He washed the hammer and returned it to the workman's bag. No suspicion fell on Jacoby but, a few days later, he gave himself up to the police.

His case caused a great deal of controversy when it was contrasted with the murder of the prostitute Olive Young in Finborough Road, Earls Court, committed that year by Ronald True. Jacoby was hanged but True, who was a forger, confidence trickster and thief, was sent to Broadmoor. The name of the hotel was later changed to the Mostyn Hotel.

The Bear Garden in the Cumberland Hotel (7) at the corner of Marble Arch was where the post-war gang leader Jack Spot held court dispensing advice and wisdom. In his brown suit, brown fedora and handmade shoes, he modelled himself on the American gangster Frank Costello. After his fight with Albert Dimes in Old Compton Street, he was again slashed, this time on 6 May 1956, outside his flat at Hyde Park Mansions.

In April 2014, Phillip Spence was charged with the murder of three women from the United Arab Emirates at the Cumberland Hotel during a robbery in which he beat them with a claw hammer while taking their gold jewellery, iPads and mobile phones. One lost an eye in the attack and all three sustained fractured skulls. In November that year, Spence was jailed for life with a minimum of eighteen years. He had amassed thirty-seven convictions going back to 1993.

An old murder, but one with an interesting legal twist, took place at 14 Norfolk Street, now known as Dunraven Street, at the northern end of Park Lane on 6 May 1840. It was there that a housemaid found the house ransacked and Lord William Russell lying dead on a bloodstained bed, his throat cut from ear to ear. There was no apparent sign of a break-in and suspicion mounted against Russell's valet, the Swiss-born François Courvoisier, particularly after some of the apparently stolen items were found hidden in the house. However, tellingly in his favour, no blood was found on him or his clothing.

Set against this was that, six weeks before the murder, Courvoisier had left a parcel with a Frenchman who ran the Dieppe Hotel off Leicester Square. Reading about the case, the owner's wife opened it and found it contained some of Lord Russell's silverware. She was taken to the prison and recognised Courvoisier.

During the trial, Courvoisier told his counsel Charles Phillips that he had, in fact, killed Russell, explaining that the absence of blood was because he had been naked at the time. Phillips went to see the judge to ask what he should do and was told that, if Courvoisier still wanted to plead not guilty, he must be allowed to do so and that Phillips must use 'all fair argument arising on the evidence'. Courvoisier was hanged on 6 July in front of a crowd of 20,000 outside the Old Bailey.

The eponymous Mount Street Bridge Club (8), also known as Leaders, was a Mayfair spieler where they played every card game – principally kalooki – except bridge. For a time, the Krays collected £20-a-week protection money from the club and it was there that 'Scotch' Jack Buggy was killed on 12 May 1967. His body, wrapped in baling wire, turned up a few days later off the south coast. The consensus of opinion was that he was also demanding protection money. In 1974, the club owner Franny Daniels, once a Jack Spot man, stood trial for the murder along with his employee Abraham Lewis. The evidence against them was mainly provided by an Australian conman-turned-informer and both were acquitted.

It was outside Claridge's in Brook Street (9) – named after Tyburn Brook, an underground river – that Detective Sergeant Harold Challoner fell from grace. A man with a fine war record who regarded himself as the scourge of the criminal classes in the West End, he was found to have planted a brick in the pocket of a man demonstrating on 11 July 1965 over the death of a Greek political activist. He was later diagnosed with paranoid schizophrenia and his colleagues at West End Central Police Station were absolved for not having realised something was wrong with his antisocial and racist behaviour. After a short spell in a mental hospital, he became a clerk to the solicitors who had represented him. Junior officers in the case were given up to three years each.

In 1849, the talented courtesan but rather less talented actress Lola Montez, mistress of Ludwig King of Bavaria, Franz Liszt and a host of others, was arrested in Half Moon Street (10), named after a pub which stood there and where the Hilton Hotel now stands, on a charge of bigamy. She had left her husband in India some years earlier and had married Guards officer George Heald at St George's, Hanover Square. She was in poor humour, principally because she had been warned of her impending arrest and was about to flee to France, but at the police station she smoked a cigar and calmed down. She eventually jumped bail and, instead of being at Marlborough Police Court for her case, she ended up with Heald in Boulogne.

The Colony Club (11) in Berkeley Square, with George Raft as the meeter and greeter, was where the Mafia set up a casino in the mid-1960s as one way of laundering their illegal profits. Over the course of a year, first Raft and then the Mafia's main man, Dino Cellini, along with several others, were expelled from or refused re-entry to Britain. The club closed before being reopened under new management.

It is said there was an underground passageway from the Colony to the Astor Club (12), to which, on a Friday, the upper echelons of the London underworld brought their girlfriends and which was generally what could be regarded as a neutral zone. However, it was there that an attempt was made in 1966 to frame Jack Spot, who had allegedly slashed another London gangster Tommy Falco. On another occasion, following a quarrel in the club, 'Mad' Frank Fraser kidnapped Eric Mason, a Kray associate, and, after taking an axe to him, deposited him outside a London hospital. When Mason asked the Krays to take punitive action on his behalf, they declined and simply gave him £40. It was at the Astor Club that the Kray Twins spent their last night of freedom before being arrested on 8 May 1968.

In 1970, eight original lithographs of the sex life of John Lennon and Yoko Ono, on show in the London Arts Gallery (13), New Bond Street, were seized on the grounds that they were obscene. A Scotland Yard officer thought they were the 'work of a sick mind' and one middle-aged housewife from Egham said she had gone 'red with embarrassment' when she saw them. The owner of the gallery was charged with exhibiting 'indecent prints' under the Metropolitan Police Act 1839 rather than the more recent Obscene Publications Act.

The Marlborough Street magistrate St John Harmsworth dismissed the case, ruling that the gallery did not constitute a thoroughfare under the terms of the 1839 Act. Had there been a conviction, there was the possibility that other art collections, including that of the Queen, might be open to prosecution.

In 1997, Russell Grant-McVicar, son of John McVicar, the notorious robber and prison escaper, went into the Lefevre Gallery (14) in Bruton Street and enquired about the price of a small Picasso oil painting *Tête de Femme*. Told it was £60,000, he produced part of a shotgun and pulled the painting from the wall. He sold the Picasso to self-styled society cat-burglar Peter Scott, who was to negotiate a ransom with the insurance company. Scott was jailed for three and a half years for handling the painting. Grant-McVicar, who defended himself at the subsequent trial, said he robbed to make 'a spiritual statement' on behalf of starving children. He had been instructed by members of 'the most powerful cult group on the planet'. He received sixteen years for this and other robberies dating back to 1993.

CHAPTER FOUR

Charing Cross and Tottenham Court Roads

Really one continuous road, Charing Cross Road runs north from St Martin-in-the-Fields to St Giles Circus where it becomes Tottenham Court Road up to the Euston Road.

The Charing Cross Road received its name from the nearby Charing Cross railway station which, in turn, took its name as the last resting place for the body of Edward I's wife, Eleanor of Castile, on its journey from Harby near Lincoln to London after she died in 1290.

In the thirteenth century, a manor house slightly north-west of what is now the corner of Tottenham Court Road and Euston Road belonged to a William de Tottenhall. In about the fifteenth century, the area was known variously as Totten, Totham, or Totting Hall. After changing hands several times, the manor was leased to Queen Elizabeth I, and it came to be popularly called Tottenham Court.

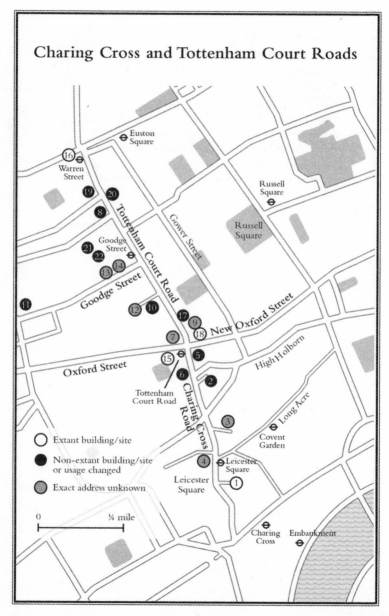

Charing Cross and Tottenham Court Roads

4. CHARING CROSS AND TOTTENHAM COURT ROADS

1. **Cecil Court**, Covent Garden.
2. **The Spanish Rooms**, Denmark Place, Soho.
3. **Flat of Madeleine Wiltshire**, Litchfield Street, Covent Garden.
4. **Mrs Fox's Restaurant**, Little Newport Street, Soho.
5. **The Artistes and Repertoire Club**, Charing Cross Road, Soho.
6. **Freddie Mills' Nitespot**, Charing Cross Road, Soho.
7. **Hayes' money-lending business**, corner of Oxford Street and Tottenham Court Road, Fitzrovia.
8. **Fairyland**, 92 Tottenham Court Road, Fitzrovia, W1T 4TL.
9. **John Starchfield**, corner of New Oxford Street and Tottenham Court Road, Fitzrovia.
10. **Carlton Picture House**, 30 Tottenham Court Road, Fitzrovia, W1T 1BX.
11. **The Bell**, 15 Little Titchfield Street, Fitzrovia, W1W.
12. **Breakfast Room Café**, Percy Street, Fitzrovia.
13. **New Court Club**, Goodge Street, Fitzrovia.
14. **Goodge Street**, Fitzrovia.
15. **Tottenham Court Road Underground station**, Oxford Street, Soho.
16. **Warren Street Underground station**, Tottenham Court Road, Bloomsbury.
17. **Luna Park**, 268-269 Tottenham Court Road, Fitzrovia, W1T 7AQ.
18. **Dominion Theatre**, 268-269 Tottenham Court Road, Fitzrovia, W1T 7AQ.
19. **Paramount Dance Hall**, 151 Tottenham Court Road, Fitzrovia, W1T 7AQ.
20. **Maples**, 149 Tottenham Court Road, Fitzrovia, W1T 7NF.
21. **Butcher Louis Voisin's flat**, 101 Charlotte Street, Fitzrovia, W1T 4QA.
22. **Scala Theatre**, 58 Charlotte Street, Fitzrovia, W1T 4ND.

Charing Cross Road has always been less associated with crime than Tottenham Court Road, but it was just off the street in Cecil Court (1) that, in 1735, Elizabeth Calloway, the owner of a brandy shop, was charged with setting fire to her stock, which she had over-insured. Calloway, who claimed that the stock had self-combusted, was acquitted. The artist William Hogarth's mother, who lodged in the basement, died in the fire.

On 3 March 1961, Elsie Batten was stabbed to death in a curio shop at 23 Cecil Court where she worked. A dress-sword was stolen and immediately sold to a gunsmith across the alleyway. He and his son gave detailed statements and, from them, an Identikit was produced of a lean-jawed Anglo-Indian which was circulated around local police stations. Five days later, a PC Cole recognised Edwin Bush from the composite image when he saw him in Old Compton Street. Bush had been in the gunsmith's shop the day before the killing enquiring how much they would pay for a sword. It was the first success the Metropolitan Police had had with an Identikit headshot, but it was actually a triumph for a variety of forensic techniques. Bush had left a clear fingerprint, palm print and shoe prints in the shop. He also had blood on his clothes. He ran an unsuccessful manslaughter defence saying that Mrs Batten had racially insulted him and he had lost his temper. He was hanged on 6 July that year.

It was to a basement in Cecil Court that the celebrated nightclub queen Kate 'Ma' Meyrick moved in 1919 from Dalton's in Leicester Square. Calling it Brett's, and with a female band with dance instructresses, Ma claimed some of her girls earned up to £80 a week and married aristocrats. She sold her share the following year and, two years later, Brett's was prosecuted when an undercover police officer saw a man pull down the top of a woman's frock without redress. There was also an allegation that a woman had been sitting with her legs crossed, so exposing her knee.

On 14 August 1980, John 'Punch' Thompson, a local petty criminal, was thrown out of the Spanish Rooms, also known as El Hueco, on the second floor of 18 Denmark Place (2), which ran off the Charing Cross Road, following a fight. Thompson returned shortly afterwards, poured petrol into the ground floor of the building and lit a match. The blaze, described as the worst fire in London in terms of loss of life since the Second World War, killed thirty-seven people from eight different nationalities – mainly Spaniards and Latin Americans – in Rodo's, another club on the first and second floors. Thompson, who claimed it was a case of mistaken identity, was convicted of murder and sentenced to life imprisonment. He died in prison in 2008 on the anniversary of the tragedy.

Blackmail has been called the 'Murder of the Soul', and in 1927, Henry Charles Wiltshire came within an ace of being charged with the murder of his wife Madeleine, his partner in the blackmail game. They had their claws into a vicar who had sensibly gone to a genuine private inquiry agent when Madeleine was found dead on 25 April in a flat in Litchfield Street (3), just below Cambridge Circus. She had been poisoned after drinking potassium cyanide disguised as tea. Two cups were found in the flat. There was some evidence that Wiltshire had bought the cyanide which, a witness claimed, he had told her was to be used as part of the coining process. He denied this, but the coroner, while calling him a liar with a cock-and-bull story, said he could not be sure who had supplied the poison or whether it was suicide, a suicide pact or, indeed, murder. Wiltshire was chased out of the court and into the street where he was attacked before the police managed to release him. The crowd then caught up with him again and were once more held back as he escaped.

In September 1920, the Jamaican drug dealer Eddie Manning received a sentence of sixteen months for shooting at three men in a fracas at Cambridge Circus on 11 July that year. If, which is doubtful, the witnesses could be relied upon, Manning had been in Mrs Fox's Restaurant in Little Newport Street (4). The eponymous Elizabeth Fox was a sort of god-mother to the underworld and, for the previous twenty years, her restaurant had been a home-from-home for out-of-work actresses, prostitutes and criminals. Always good for advice and, better still, a hand-out, she was sorely missed when she went to America where she died of cancer.

Things had been peaceful that afternoon until a pimp, 'Yankee Frank' Miller, who had just been acquitted at the Old Bailey of burglary, tried to blag a pound from Manning and then hit and threw a lit cigar in the face of a girl, Molly O'Brien, who had apparently interfered. Manning chased after Miller and shot at him and his companions. Far more likely, though, the quarrel was over the division of drug profits.

It was Manning's first conviction and Mr Justice Greer

took the view he had been more sinned against than sinning, saying how much he regretted having to sentence a man of respectable character but that foreigners had to be taught that guns could not be discharged on London's streets.

The Artistes and Repertoire club (5) – known as the A&R – was in a building almost opposite what was once the Astoria at the north end of the Charing Cross Road. At one time the A&R was owned by the footballer Malcolm Allison who was helped out by the Scotland and Arsenal star Jimmy Logie, but in its heyday in the 1960s it was owned by Mickey Regan and Ronnie Knight, then the husband of Barbara Windsor, with Regan's brother Brian on the door. It was the drinking establishment of choice for some of the musicians from Tin Pan Alley, as well as actors such as Kenneth Williams, Ian Hendry and Ronnie Fraser. It also became a home-from-home for some of London's most notorious villains, including the balding, unassuming-looking Jimmy Essex, one of the few men acquitted twice for murder.

Marilyn Wisbey, daughter of Tommy Wisbey, the Great Train Robber, recalled:

'I would say it was the best afternoon drinker, especially on Mondays and Fridays. There were more piss-artists and reps (as in salesmen) in there than any other club I know. Singers and musicians would be allowed to get up and play. Then there would be all different firms popping in and out, and also madams. There was one who used to have apartments all over London . . . "Mary from the Dairy" she was known as.'

The club became something like the boots in the film *All Quiet on the Western Front*, passing from one owner and one misfortune to the next. After Ronnie Knight disposed of the club, James Fraser, the nephew of 'Mad' Frank Fraser, took over and, in turn, it was bought by Georgie Stokes. Unfortunately, Stokes forgot to renew the licence and the authorities closed it down. Stokes was later arrested over a cocaine deal and received a twelve-year sentence. In 1991, he escaped from Maidstone Prison and was found in Trinidad five years later. James Fraser was killed in 2004 in a street accident when he took his family on holiday to Florida. For years, the club has remained empty.

Almost opposite the A&R was the once fashionable Freddie Mills Chinese Restaurant, later Freddie Mills' Nitespot (6), which Mills ran in partnership with Andy Ho. There is only one thing on which people can agree about the death of Mills, a one-time light heavyweight champion of the world and television celebrity. That is that, on the night of 25 July 1965, he was found shot in the eye in his car parked in Goslett Yard at the back of his club. Apart from that fact, many questions arise: was it suicide or murder, and why? Why would Freddie, one of the most popular figures of his day, want to kill himself? Why would anyone want to kill him?

Most nights of the week, Mills would drive to the club from his home in Denmark Hill, south London, and would often have a sleep in his car parked in the yard. When law student Robert Deacon, the club's part-time doorman, went to wake him at a quarter to midnight, he realised something was seriously wrong and raised the alarm. The air rifle used, which Mills had borrowed from a friend, was still in the car.

The police, pathologist Professor Keith Simpson, and the coroner Gavin Thurston were all convinced it had, indeed, been suicide. Simpson thought the wounds were caused by 'deliberate self-infliction'. This left the question of why he had killed himself. Certainly, he was having money troubles and had been liquidating his considerable assets; in addition, the club was not doing well and there were suggestions that Andy Ho had been raiding the till. There were also allegations that Mills was a homosexual, and that he had been caught in a public lavatory shortly before his death, or that he was 'Jack the Stripper', a murderer of prostitutes in the Hammersmith area, and the net was closing in. Others were convinced he was killed for refusing to pay protection money or that Triads wanted to take over his club because Goslett Yard had an exit in both the Charing Cross Road and Oxford Street, which would facilitate drug deals. It was even suggested that he was killed by Mafia hitmen on the orders of Meyer Lansky, because he was trying to blackmail the boxing promoter and Mafia associate Benny Huntsman into lending him money.

In 1726, Catharine Hayes – whose husband had a chandlery and money-lending business on the corner of Tottenham Court Road (7) and what was then Tyburn Road, now Oxford Street – persuaded two of her lovers, Thomas Wood and Thomas Billings, who was reputedly her son, to help her murder him over the substantial sum of £500. John Hayes was butchered and his head was thrown into the Thames. After it washed up three weeks later, it was a simple question of identification. All three were found guilty of murder and additionally she was convicted of petty treason because the Treason Act 1351 included the killing of a husband by his wife. Punishment for Petty Treason was much more severe than for 'ordinary' murderers, with convicted women being burned at the stake up to 1793.

Wood died in prison on the morning of his execution, and Hayes was the last woman to be burned at the stake. The hangman failed to strangle her and she was literally roasted alive. Billings was later hanged in Marylebone Fields.

With transatlantic crossing time rapidly improving at the end of the nineteenth century, a number of high-class American criminals came to London. They included Annie Gleason, who sometimes represented herself as the daughter of President Ulysses S. Grant.

The diminutive American conwoman first appeared at the London Sessions for an attempted theft from Christie's in 1905, when she received three years. In January 1909, she married an American, Theodore Albert Gillespie, who was one half of comic duo Ferguson and Mack, and they lived together at 34 Little Newport Street. It was a bigamous marriage because her real husband, Mickey Gleason, was then serving a sentence in Munich. Two years later, she received five years for theft, again at the London Sessions. Gillespie visited her in the cells but died of a broken heart (she said) within a month.

But her real downfall came when on 23 April 1915 she was back at the Old Bailey along with another American, Charlie Allen. This time it was a robbery with violence of a jeweller, Wladyslaw Gutowski, from Percy Street, Tottenham Court Road, when they cleared some £600 worth of gems. She had already had dealings with the jeweller, having bought a small diamond ring from him for £27 as part of the set-up. Now she told him that she was being kept in style by an English gentleman who wanted to buy her some valuable diamonds. At the time she was staying at the Savoy Mansions where, some years later, the actress Billie Carlton would kill herself on the night of the Victory Ball.

On 10 February, the jeweller dutifully appeared for the appointment. He was sandbagged and then chloroformed by a Russian helpmate posing as a page. Allen was the look-out man. When the police searched the flat, they found a lady's silk handkerchief in a drawer and Gleason was traced through the laundry mark. None of the gems were recovered.

At least in court, Gleason and Allen were given their due when they were described as 'two of the most dangerous thieves in the world' and, in her case, as 'looked upon as one of the most successful American thieves we have here today'. Allen received twelve years and twelve strokes of the cat. Gleason was sentenced to ten years and, as she left the dock, 'looked reproachfully' at Mr Justice Lawrence. Allen died in prison; Gleason was released on licence in January 1923 and died twelve years later in Chicago.

In the period leading up to and during the First World War, Fairyland (8), an amusement arcade at 92 Tottenham Court Road, was run by Henry Stanton Morley. Apart from a guess-your-weight machine, a small skittle alley and a fortune teller, on the top floor was what was advertised as 'London's premier revolver gun shooting gallery'. It was here that members of the Indian Abhinav Bharat Society, which believed in armed revolution, practised for their proposed assassinations. On 1 July 1909, in the hours before Madan Lal Dhingra killed Sir William Hutt Curzon Wyllie and Cawas Lalcaca, who tried to stop him, at the Imperial Institute in South Kensington, he had been practising at the gallery, hitting the target with eleven out of twelve shots at a range of 18ft. Justice was swift in those days and Dhingra was hanged at Pentonville a month later. That year, the owner, Henry Morley, reported that the range was being used by two suffragettes who brought along their own state-of-the-art Browning revolver. It was thought to be possibly a conspiracy to assassinate the Prime Minister Herbert Asquith.

On 12 August 1914, one of the earliest First World War deserters, Donald Lesbini, shot and killed Alice Storey who worked at Fairyland. Lesbini, of Greek origin, had taken offence when she called him 'Ikey', a reference to his Jewish looks, which he resented. He was convicted and sentenced to death, but was reprieved. In prison, his mental condition deteriorated and in 1931 he was sent to Broadmoor. He was released in 1939.

On 27 September 1913, John Starchfield, a newspaper seller near the corner of New Oxford Street and Tottenham Court Road (9), became a local hero when he and George Holding chased after and caught Stephen Titus, an Armenian who had shot and killed Esther Towers, the manageress of the nearby Horseshoe Hotel. Starchfield was shot in the stomach, but Holding managed to get the man's gun away and the crowd joined in to capture him. Starchfield was awarded £50 for his bravery and a pension of a week from the Carnegie Trust. The coroner's jury divided their fees between Holding and

Starchfield's wife, and Holding received an additional £5 from the Bow Street magistrate along with a postal order for 2s 6d sent to the court.

It was a case of hero to nearly zero. On 9 January 1914, the body of Starchfield's seven-year-old son William was found on a train at Shoreditch. He had been strangled, and the medical evidence was that he had been killed between 2.00 and 3.00 p.m. after his mother sent him out on an errand. Starchfield, who was separated from his wife, was arrested and committed for trial.

One piece of evidence was that of a signalman who said he could identify Starchfield from a distance of twenty-five yards over a period of ten seconds. Other witnesses said they had seen him with his son in Endell Street. He had an alibi in the form of a hotel porter who said he had seen Starchfield in bed. He did not need the alibi. On the second day, the trial judge suggested the prosecution abandon the case. The most likely explanation is that the boy was killed by a maniac. There is, however, a suggestion that a friend of Titus's killed the boy by way of revenge. Starchfield died from the effects of the shooting injury two years after his son.

The old Carlton Picture House (10) at 30 Tottenham Court Road opened in 1913 showing *Germinal*, directed by Albert Capellani. Underneath was Rector's Dance Hall, a club in which the licensing authorities took a close interest and which was described by an inquiry agent as where 'rich male customers are fleeced by wily hostesses'. The jazz musician Sidney Bechet played there when he visited London after the First World War. He drank in The Bell (11) in Little Titchfield

Street, one of the few pubs which welcomed black men. The landlady, Mary Rose Kildare, had married the black saxophonist Daniel Kildare, but in June 1920 he killed his then estranged wife and her sister as well as a barmaid and then shot himself.

In the early hours of 2 September 1922, Bechet and a friend met Ruby Gordon and Pauline Lampe, who claimed they were dancers – Bechet said Gordon was a prostitute whom he had frequented before – at the Breakfast Room Café (12) in Percy Street and took them back to Bechet's rooms. It was there, claimed Gordon, that both men assaulted her. She said Bechet had pushed her on to a bed and tried to strip her. Bechet said the quarrel had arisen when he would not take drugs from her. Both men received fourteen days, upheld on appeal, and Bechet was deported. He was not allowed to return to England until 1931.

After the war, the Carlton reopened as the Berkeley, showing risqué continental films. The dance hall was again called Rector's before it became the Blarney Dance Hall. It lacked real soundproofing and audiences upstairs watching delicate moments in French films could often hear '*Dozy-do yer partners all . . . rub their bellies with linseed oil . . .*' or similar. It closed in August 1976. A major redevelopment of the area took place and it is now the site of the present Odeon cinema.

On 6 March 1922, a dancing instructress, Freda Kempton, was found dead from an overdose of cocaine. She was to have married a Manchester businessman on the Monday after her death, and a friend recalled that she had promised to give up dancing after her fiancé had sent her money for clothes for the wedding. And on this occasion, the notorious drug dealer

Brilliant Chang made another appearance. He had met Freda and her friend Rose Heinberg in the New Court Club (13) off Tottenham Court Road the night before. The next day, Freda had suffered from a splitting headache and had gone into convulsions. At the inquest, Chang faced a hostile series of questions. The story from Rose Heinberg was that Freda had asked him if anyone had died from sniffing cocaine and he had replied that the only way to kill oneself was to put it in water. 'She was a friend of mine, but I know nothing about the cocaine,' he told the coroner. He had given her money but not drugs. 'It is all a mystery to me.'

When the fashionable preacher William Dodd was hanged for the forgery of a bond of £4,200 on 27 June 1777, his body was rushed to the house of Davies, an undertaker in Goodge Street (14) off Tottenham Court Road, where 'it was placed in a hot bath, and every exertion made to restore life, but in vain'. It was about Dodd's confession that Samuel Johnson made his famous remark: 'Depend upon it, Sir, when a man knows he is to be hanged in a fortnight, it concentrates his mind wonderfully.'

Immediately prior to the Second World War, there was a wave of IRA bomb attacks and, on 4 February 1939, both Tottenham Court Road (15) and Leicester Square Underground stations were blown up. There were no deaths but two people were severely injured when suitcase bombs stored in left-luggage rooms overnight exploded.

During the Blitz, Warren Street Underground station (16) at the Euston end of Tottenham Court Road was used as an overnight air-raid shelter and it was certainly possible to get a good night's sleep there.

In 1943, the burglar Harold Loughans used people sleeping there as his alibi when he was accused of the murder of Rose Robinson, who had run the John Barleycorn Public House in Portsmouth, after she had been found strangled in her bedroom. They said they had seen him before they went to sleep and he was still in bed in the morning. In fact, he had crept out, driven to Portsmouth and was back before dawn while they were still asleep. He was acquitted but later confessed to the murder.

After the war, Warren Street was one of the great streets for buying used cars. The London gangster Frank Fraser recalled:

'They'd have cars in showrooms and parked on the pavement. There could be up to fifty cars and, then again, some people would just stand on the pavement and pass on the info that there was a car to sell.

'Warren Street was mostly for mug punters. Chaps wouldn't buy one. People would come down from as far away as Scotland to buy a car. All polished and shiny with the clock turned back and the insides hanging out.

And if you bought a car and it fell to bits, who was you going to complain to?'

Parking wardens and regulations by the council eventually put an end to car dealing in Warren Street.

At Luna Park (17), where the Dominion now stands, the main attraction in pre-war years was the 'Human Seal', a woman dressed in a spangled costume and a Neptune helmet who nightly would wrap herself in cotton wool, set fire to herself and then dive into a water tank.

On 21 October 1954, the London gang leader Jack Spot (Comer) beat up the newspaper reporter Duncan Webb at the back of the Dominion (18). Webb had aligned himself with Spot's onetime friend now rival Billy Hill, who had been harassing him. Webb received a call from a man called Nadel, saying he must meet him urgently, but when he arrived on the steps of the Dominion, he found it was Spot, who took him into an alley and knocked him down, breaking his wrist. Webb was paid off privately with £600 to reduce a charge of grievous bodily harm and Spot was fined £50, but that did not stop Webb suing him over his broken wrist. He was awarded £732 and, when Spot refused to pay, Webb had him made bankrupt.

Also in Tottenham Court Road was the Paramount Dance Hall (19) – known as London's Harlem – where, in 1939, the capital's first Jitterbug competition was held. The newspapers were critical – nine out of ten of the men were Afro-Americans and almost all the girls were white. It later became known as the Empire Rooms.

In September 1953, the burglar Alfie Hinds was convicted of a robbery at Maples (20), almost opposite Warren Street station. The conviction was mainly reliant on the bitterly contested evidence of Chief Superintendent Herbert Sparks, who claimed to have found dust from the department store in Hinds' trouser turn-ups, something which Hinds said had been planted by him. A very hostile Lord Goddard gave him twelve years.

Throughout his sentence Hinds repeatedly escaped, taking the opportunity to proclaim his innocence while on the run. Then, on his retirement, Sparks published his memoirs in the

People, saying Hinds couldn't admit he'd been out-thought by the police: 'I think it is a pity Alfie could not take his medicine manfully'. It was a good time for Hinds to bring an action. The Metropolitan Police were in disgrace, with detectives from West End Central accused of planting evidence. He sued for libel. Sparks did not make a good witness and suffered under cross-examination. Despite another adverse summing-up, the jury awarded Hinds £300.

Against his barrister's advice, Hinds went back to the Court of Appeal which upheld the conviction. The general feeling in the underworld was that Sparks had indeed planted the evidence and that Hinds had indeed committed the robbery. The law was changed shortly after to prevent others like Hinds suing in the civil courts to try to overturn a criminal conviction.

Hinds, a member of MENSA, later went on to lecture in criminology and became a successful property developer. Sparks died a bitter man warning other ex-officers against publishing their memoirs.

Parallel to Tottenham Court Road is Charlotte Street where in 1917, at number 101 (21), a cask containing Émillienne Gérard's head and hands was found in a basement flat belonging to Soho butcher Louis Voisin. Her torso and arms had already been found in Regent Square wrapped in a paper meat sack with 'Blodie Belgian' written on it. It had been traced through a laundry mark to 50 Munster Square where there was a photograph of Voisin on the mantelpiece.

It seems Voisin had had two mistresses and Gérard had turned up uninvited when he was in bed with Berthe Roche.

Some of the most damning evidence against him was that when he was asked to write 'Bloody Belgian' he wrote the words as they were on the brown paper. Although it seems likely that Berthe struck the fatal blow – Voisin was far too strong to have done so little damage to Gérard's skull – he took full blame at the trial and Mr Justice Darling sentenced him to death – in French. Roche died two years into a seven-year sentence for being an accessory after the fact.

On 29 April 1947, Alec de Antiquis was killed when he tried to prevent robbers escaping from Jay's Jewellers near what used to be the Scala Theatre (22) in Charlotte Street. The raid itself had been a total failure. While the staff were being held at gunpoint, one employee managed to press the burglar alarm and a director, Ernest Stock, managed to shut the safe. Then seventy-year-old Bertram Keates threw a stool at the robbers and, after a shot was fired at him, the men ran out into the street. Unfortunately for them, a lorry was blocking their Vauxhall getaway car and they set off on foot waving their guns.

It was a time when passers-by would 'have a go', and the gang was first chased by Charles Grimshaw. Then thirty-four-year-old father-of-six Alec de Antiquis tried to block their path by stalling his motorbike, and was shot for his pains. As he lay dying, he said, 'I tried to stop them. I did my best . . .'

The robbers were Harry 'Harry Boy' Jenkins, Christopher Geraghty and seventeen-year-old Terence Rolt. They were traced through a raincoat found in a room in Tottenham Court Road which had been bought by Jenkins' brother-in-law from a shop in Deptford. Jenkins, known as 'The King of Borstal', had only been released six days before the robbery. Another man, William Wilson, admitted casing the shop. He denied being on the robbery but named Jenkins.

The first to confess was Geraghty, who named Rolt, who in turn named Jenkins. It seems that the bungling of the raid had been the fault of Rolt who had been told to wait outside; however, he had decided to follow the others into the shop. But it was Geraghty who had shot de Antiquis. He and Jenkins were hanged on 19 September 1947.

After Geraghty's execution, the Governor of Pentonville Prison apparently wrote to Jenkins' mother saying she could not have his clothes since he had been hanged in them but she could, if she wished, have his belt, braces and shoelaces.

CHAPTER FIVE

Regent Street

Originally called New Street and then renamed after the Prince Regent (later George IV), Regent Street was built under the direction of the architect John Nash. From top to bottom, Regent Street runs from All Souls Church at the northern end through Piccadilly Circus to Waterloo Place in St James's at the southern end.

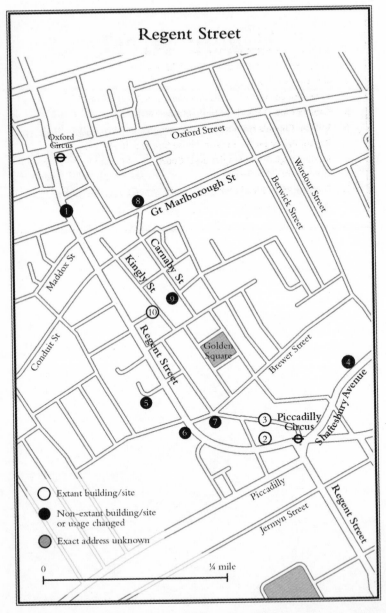

Regent Street

Extant building/site

Non-extant building/site
or usage changed

Exact address unknown

0   ¼ mile

5. REGENT STREET

1. **Jay's**, 243 Regent Street, Mayfair, W1B 2EN.
2. **Café Royal**, 68 Regent Street, Soho, W1B 4DY.
3. **Glasshouse Street**, Soho.
4. **Café Monico**, 39-45 Shaftesbury Avenue, Soho, W1D 6LA.
5. **Cabinet Club**, 9 Heddon Street, Mayfair, W1B 4BE.
6. **Brilliant Chang's restaurant**, 107 Regent Street, Mayfair, W1B 4HL.
7. **Regent Palace Hotel**, 33 Glasshouse Street, Soho, W1B 5RD.
8. **Marlborough Street Magistrates' Court**, 19–21 Great Marlborough Street, Soho, W1F 7HL.
9. **Florence Mills Social Club**, 50 Carnaby Street, Soho, W1F 9QA.
10. **Emporium nightclub**, 10 Kingly Street, Soho, W1B 5PJ.

Throughout the nineteenth century, Regent Street was known as the haunt of prostitutes and, in June 1887, Elizabeth Cass found to her cost that single women should not go there after 10.00 p.m. without risk of arrest. She had just bought a pair of gloves at Jay's (1) at 243 Regent Street when she was arrested and charged with soliciting. The officer said he had seen her regularly over the previous weeks. Despite her employer telling the magistrate Robert Newton that the girl had not been out of the house on any evening, he convicted her. A subsequent hearing cleared the officer of perjury but he was shuffled off to work at the British Museum.

Seven years later, the problem of prostitutes still persisted and, in 1894, a man complained to *The Times* that, unless he was in company with his daughter, he could not walk down the street without being accosted. A later correspondent advised him that Regent Street was by no means as bad as Leicester Square.

Then, on 1 May 1905, came one of the earliest twentieth-century Metropolitan Police scandals when a French woman, Eva D'Angeley, was arrested for 'riotous and indecent' behaviour in Regent Street. The charge was dismissed after a Mr D'Angeley told the stipendiary magistrate that he was married to the lady and that she was merely waiting for him. Better still, Sub-Divisional Inspector MacKay told the court he believed them to be a respectable married couple. So, amidst allegations of corruption, police harassment and bribery, a Royal Commission was established into methods and discipline in the force.

The D'Angeley case was one of nineteen selected for

examination by the Commissioners and now rather different facts began to emerge. MacKay claimed that Greek Street 'is one of the very worst streets I have to deal with. In fact, it is the worst street in the West End of London.' He had made further enquiries into Mrs D'Angeley and her husband and now realised he had been over-generous towards the pair. They had retreated to Paris with such speed that they had forgotten to pack their trunks which they left behind, as well as forgetting to pay the rent on their lodgings. Unsurprisingly, offers by the Commission to pay their fares back to London were ignored.

The case threw up all sorts of questions about MacKay. How could an experienced officer not recognise a French pimp? Why did he not ask the magistrate for a short adjournment to make proper enquiries? But as is so often the case, much of the report was a whitewash. The Commission found that 'the Metropolitan Police is entitled to the confidence of all classes of the community'.

The Café Royal (2) at the southern end of Nash's colonnaded terraces was opened in 1865 by Frenchman Daniel Thévenon who had fled France when he was made bankrupt. In 1892, Oscar Wilde and Lord Alfred Douglas had been lunching there when Wilde invited the Marquess of Queensberry to join them. Things had been cordial and the Marquess had invited Wilde to stay with him in Torquay.

On 24 March 1895, the Irish writer Frank Harris advised Oscar Wilde to drop his charge of criminal libel against the Marquess of Queensberry who had left a card with the hall porter at the Albemarle addressed to Wilde, 'posing as a somdomite [sic]'. Wilde ignored the advice. Queensberry was acquitted, and Wilde was subsequently tried, convicted and imprisoned.

The Frenchman Marius Martin, who was a night porter at the Café Royal, was found beaten to death in Glasshouse Street (3) on 6 December the previous year at the back of the restaurant. One possible motive was robbery, but he was also deeply unpopular with other members of the staff whom he had reported for taking home leftover food. No one was ever charged. Another less probable suggestion was that he was killed because of his opposition to the Irish Fenian movement.

In 1910, the Australian Daniel Melaney was sentenced to five years for distributing the proceeds of a spectacular jewel theft at the nearby Café Monico (4), owned by Giacomo and Battista Monico, then a home-away-from-home for Australian confidence men, where they hosted a dinner for the visiting Australian detective Chief Inspector Harry Mann. The robbery was organised by the great East London receiver and putter-up Joseph 'Cammi' Grizzard. The target, the French jeweller Frederick Goldschmidt, was followed from Paris with a bag containing something in the region of £60,000 worth of jewellery by at least two teams working without the other's knowledge. Goldschmidt stayed at De Keyser's Hotel on the Embankment and it became apparent that the only time he put his bag down was when he washed his hands.

On 9 July, in the washroom of the Café Monico, when he reached for the soap he was pushed off balance and the bag was snatched by the extremely nimble ex-jockey Harry Grimshaw. A story is told that when the police searched Grizzard's home that evening he hid a diamond necklace from the haul, which he had yet to fence, in a bowl of pea soup. Other accounts have it that it was taken out by a maid as the police arrived and, more engagingly, that the necklace was hidden in Mrs Grizzard's underwear, somewhere the delicate-minded police of the day would not dare to search.

The first London nightclub was opened in 1912 at 9 Heddon Street just off Regent Street by Frida Strindberg, in the year her husband, the Swedish playwright August, died. The Cabinet Club (5), always known as the Golden Calf, in the basement of a cloth-seller's, was intended to recreate the cabarets of Vienna. Although its patrons included the sculptor Jacob Epstein, the painter Augustus John, the poet Ezra Pound and the writer Wyndham Lewis – described by Ernest Hemingway as 'having the eyes of an unsuccessful rapist' – it was not a financial success. It closed two years later after a police raid. Mrs Strindberg was fined £60 with two months in default of payment for selling liquor without a licence and, disillusioned, she sailed for New York. But it lit the way. By the 1920s there were more than fifty cabaret and dance clubs in Soho and the West End and, with their more or less complete disregard for the licensing laws, they were a constant problem for the authorities.

The year after Frida Strindberg opened her club, the drug dealer Chan Nan opened his restaurant at 107 Regent Street (6). One of the first and certainly the best known of the major Chinese drug dealers, Chan Nan, known as Brilliant Chang, was scarcely 5ft tall and wore patent leather shoes and a fur-collared Melton cloth coat. He described himself as a general merchant and an Admiralty contractor, and was referred to by the *Daily Express* as 'the unemotional yellow man, his narrow slit eyes blank, his face a mask'.

Chang, apparently the son of a well-to-do businessman, had been sent to England to pursue a commercial career or study medicine – accounts vary. Instead, he opened his restaurant and started drug trafficking on the side from his private suite. In a short time he was regarded as the leader of drug traffickers in the West End. White women fascinated him and he also trafficked in them. Those who attracted him would receive a pre-printed note via a waiter inviting them to join him. Curiously, although the recipients could not possibly have thought they had suddenly induced an irresistible urge in Mr Chang to write to them, he had a high success rate. From there, it was often a short step to drugs and degradation.

In the late 1920s, Colonel Leslie Ivor Victor Gauntlett Bligh Barker ran a restaurant, hunted and boxed while having some spare time to be a leading light in the National Fascist party. It was only after the good Colonel's arrest at the Regent Palace Hotel (7) close to Piccadilly Circus on bankruptcy charges and his subsequent examination in the reception area of Brixton Prison that he was hastily shuffled off to Holloway – a women's prison – from where she was released after a day. Unfortunately, the damage had been done and the Colonel now appeared at the Old Bailey charged with causing a false entry to be made in a marriage register.

She had been married as a woman and, towards the end of the First World War, had had two children by an Australian who had left her. She had then adopted men's clothing, gazetted herself (made public announcements about her whereabouts) and taken a title. Thinking it better for her son Tony, to whom she was devoted, to have a woman's influence, she married a chemist's daughter, Elfrieda Hayward. A lack of sexual intercourse was explained away by war injuries.

At the Old Bailey, she offered the sad explanation that 'the world offers more opportunities for advancement to a man than it does to a woman'. Unfortunately, she found the Recorder of London, Sir Ernest Wild, in an intransigent mood: he sentenced her to nine months' imprisonment before taking her counsel Henry Curtis-Bennett back to his room. There he explained his reasoning behind the judgment: 'I sentenced her for the profanation of holy matrimony and for her unfeminine conduct. She outraged the decency of nature and broke the law of man.' Wild then read Curtis-Bennett some of his poetry.

Wild conjured up some splendid pronouncements while on the bench. One of his better ones when dealing with a gross indecency case was, 'As long as I sit in this exalted seat I will cleanse the public urinals of our great Metropolis with the utmost vigour and determination.'

'Colonel' Barker's son was killed in the war without knowing that his father was indeed his mother, and she went to live, again as a man, in a village in Suffolk where she died in 1960.

Running off Regent Street close to Oxford Circus is Great Marlborough Street, named after the first Duke and commemorating his four victories in the War of the Spanish Succession. In 1760, the madam Charlotte Hayes opened a 'nunnery' in the street and, with some of the profits, her partner Dennis O'Kelly bought the great racehorse Eclipse which sired three

Derby winners, two of which were also owned by O'Kelly. He died a rich man but she wasted her money and, by 1798, she was in a debtors' prison.

At number 21 Great Marlborough Street (8), the second oldest magistrates' court in the United Kingdom – while not the equal of Bow Street for celebrated clients – nevertheless heard a number of famous cases. They included those of the Soho pimps the Messina brothers and, later, of Mick Jagger and Keith Richards, both fined on drugs charges.

It was from Marlborough Street court cells that the transvestite and expert lock-picker David Martin, charged with shooting at a policeman, escaped on Christmas Eve 1982. He was not recaptured until the following March in a tunnel at Belsize Park Underground station. He later committed suicide in prison following a row over what programme should be on the communal television. The court closed in 1998 and was later reopened as the Courthouse Hotel.

In a very curious case, the crusading journalist Duncan Webb – who was a one-man campaigner against organised vice and is sometimes credited with coining the phrase 'she offered me vice services but I made my excuses and left' – once appeared at Marlborough Street Magistrates' Court on charges of grievous bodily harm and impersonating a police officer. He had, so the court was told by a prostitute, Jean Crews, agreed to have intercourse with her for £2. They had what she quaintly described as 'connections' and he subsequently went to the bathroom to 'cleanse himself'. It was after that that he refused to leave the flat. She said she would call the police and he left with her. In the street, they encountered a Herbert Gardner Wadham, and Webb showed him his press card, masking it so it appeared to be a police warrant card. He seems to have arrested Wadham and then hit him in the face. As they marched along Tottenham Court Road, Wadham approached a temporary reserve policeman and asked for help.

At the police station, Webb denied ever having seen Wadham. The grievous bodily harm charge was reduced to one of common assault and he was bound over in the sum of two guineas under the Prosecution of Offences Act. The charge of impersonating a police officer was dismissed.

In offices almost opposite number 21 was the fashionable, if thoroughly dishonest, solicitor Arthur Newton who represented the murderer Dr Crippen. Newton always wore grey silk gloves because, he said, it was impossible when dealing with criminal cases to keep his hands clean. He was jailed for six months for trying to spirit witnesses out of the country before they could be called to give evidence in the Cleveland Street Brothel case in which Prince Albert, the Duke of Clarence, was rumoured to have been involved. He later sold a completely false confession by Crippen to the *Evening Times*, the fallout from which ruined the paper and for which the Law Society suspended Newton.

He was barely back in practice when, in 1913, he was charged over a Canadian land swindle and went to prison for three years. Later, he opened a matrimonial agency matching wealthy Americans with the daughters of titled but impoverished Englishmen.

In the 1960s, Carnaby Street – parallel to Regent Street – became the symbol of a rejuvenated and swinging London.

For a hundred years it had been much as described by Charles Dickens in *Nicholas Nickleby*, as a 'bygone, faded, tumbledown street with the irregular rows of tall, meagre houses'.

In the 1930s, the street was the home of a number of jazz clubs, including the Florence Mills Social Club (9) at number 50, opened by Amy Ashwood Garvey, the first wife of the Jamaican political leader Marcus Garvey, and her then companion, the Trinidadian musician Sam Manning. It quickly became known as a place for supporters of Pan-Africanism – a belief that African peoples, both on the continent and in the diaspora, share not merely a common history, but a common destiny. The club was named after the black singer and dancer who had starred in the 1926 show *Blackbirds*; her song, 'I'm a Little Blackbird', was a plea for racial equality.

By the 1940s, however, the club had passed through the hands of various owners and was now regarded as a home of the underworld and of prostitutes where guns were handed in with hats and coats at the door. It was now called the Blue Lagoon Club. Elizabeth Jones was what was called an exotic dancer in the Blue Lagoon before, in October 1944, she met Karl Hulten, an American Army deserter who had promoted himself to lieutenant. On their second date in a stolen lorry, she told Hulten she would like to be a real gun moll and, together, they knocked a girl off her bicycle and stole a few shillings. After a series of petty crimes, they robbed and shot taxi driver George Heath. Both were convicted; Hulten was hanged and, after her reprieve, bitterly opposed by women in particular, Jones served nine years.

Shortly after the Second World War, there was a spate

of prostitute murders in and around Soho. The first, on 10 November 1946, was the 31-year-old ex-Borstal girl Margaret Cook. Another exotic dancer, she was shot outside the Blue Lagoon a little before 9.00 p.m. She was heard to say to her killer, 'I know you have a gun. Put it away.' The man, wearing a pork-pie hat and a Burberry-style raincoat, was chased but disappeared into a crowd near Oxford Circus Tube station.

The police issued the description of a man they wished to question but with no success. Then, apart from saying they thought the killer came from Scotland, their enquiries died down. It was not until 2015 that a 91-year-old man went into a police station in Ontario and showed officers there a gun which, he said, he had used to kill a woman. His conscience had been troubling him and, since he had cancer, he wished to clear things up. He could not remember the name of the woman but he picked out Cook from a series of photographs.

In 1998, Paul 'Paddlefoot' Anthony received eighteen years for shooting an innocent stranger in the crowded Emporium nightclub (10) towards the Oxford Circus end of Regent Street. Two weeks before Christmas 1997, 43-year-old father-of-two Tony Smith went to the club to join a private party. Anthony, together with another man who was never arrested, appeared and shot him three times from a range of 6ft. Amazingly, Smith survived.

The shooting had all the hallmarks of a drug gang execution but Tony Smith had absolutely no criminal connections. In fact, Gilbert Wynter, an enforcer for a north London family, had commissioned the hit with a figure of £300 as the price quoted and, inadvisedly, he had chosen Anthony, a known drug addict.

However, the police believed that Anthony had deliberately opted to shoot the wrong man when he found out who the real target was intended to be: he dared not shoot the man, said to be from a major west London family, for fear of an inevitable reprisal. On the other hand, he could not go back to Wynter and his employers having refused to carry out the hit. The only solution was to murder somebody else, and he all but succeeded.

CHAPTER SIX

Hyde Park to Leicester Square

Hyde Park, the largest of the four royal parks, derives its name from the Hyde, an ancient manor of the priory of Westminster.

The name Piccadilly dates from 1743 and comes from a 'piccadill', the wide, often lace-decorated collar fashionable in the seventeenth century and designed by Robert Baker.

Coventry Street, named after Henry Coventry, Secretary of State to Charles II, runs from Piccadilly Circus to Leicester Square and for such a short street it has packed in more than its fair share of bad behaviour – than many a longer one.

Leicester Square, laid out in 1670, was named after the contemporary Leicester House, itself named after Robert Sidney, 2nd Earl of Leicester.

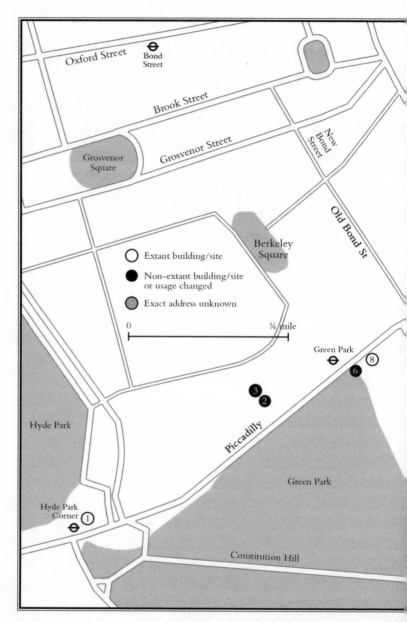

Oxford Street

Bond Street

Brook Street

Grosvenor Street

New Bond Street

Grosvenor Square

Berkeley Square

Old Bond St

○ Extant building/site

● Non-extant building/site or usage changed

● Exact address unknown

0   ¼ mile

Green Park

⑧

⑥

❸ ❷

Hyde Park

Piccadilly

Green Park

Hyde Park Corner ①

Constitution Hill

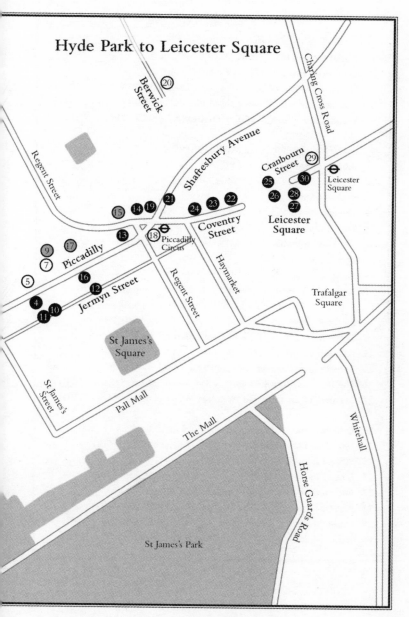

Hyde Park to Leicester Square

Berwick Street

⑳

Shaftesbury Avenue

Charing Cross Road

Cranbourn Street

㉙

㉚

㉕

Leicester Square

㉖ ㉘
㉗

Leicester Square

㉑

㉔ ㉓ ㉒

Coventry Street

⑮ ⑭ ⑲

Regent Street

⑬

⑨ ⑰

⑱

Piccadilly Circus

Regent Street

Haymarket

⑦

Piccadilly

⑯

⑤

⑫

Jermyn Street

④ ⑩

Trafalgar Square

⑪

St James's Square

St James's Street

Pall Mall

The Mall

Whitehall

Horse Guards Road

St James's Park

6. HYDE PARK TO LEICESTER SQUARE

1. **Apsley House**, 149 Piccadilly, Mayfair, W1J 7NT.
2. **Cambridge House**, 94 Piccadilly, Mayfair, W1J 7BP.
3. **Naval and Military Club**, 94 Piccadilly, Mayfair, W1J 7BP.
4. **The Egyptian Hall**, 172 Piccadilly, St James's, W1J 9EJ.
5. **Burlington House and Burlington Arcade**, Piccadilly, Mayfair, W1J 0BD.
6. **Bath House**, 82 Piccadilly, Mayfair, W1J 9DZ.
7. **Albany, Piccadilly**, Mayfair, W1J 0HF.
8. **The Ritz**, 150 Piccadilly, St James's, W1J 9BR.
9. **Sackville Street**, Mayfair.
10. **The Society**, 49 Jermyn Street, St James's, SW1Y 6LX.
11. **The 55 Club**, 55 Jermyn Street, St James's, SW1Y 6LX.
12. **The Turkish Baths**, 92 Jermyn Street, St James's, W1J 7NF.
13. **Thomas Hardy**, 9 Piccadilly, Mayfair, W1J 0DD.
14. **Abingdon House**, Piccadilly Circus, Soho.
15. **Birthplace of Horatia Nelson**, Piccadilly near Air Street, Mayfair.
16. **Pigalle restaurant**, 196 Piccadilly, St James's, W1J 9EU.
17. **Swallow Street**, Mayfair.
18. **Shaftesbury Memorial Fountain of Anteros**, Piccadilly Circus, Soho.
19. **Rainbow Corner**, 23 Shaftesbury Avenue, Piccadilly, W1D 7EE.
20. **Berwick Street market**, Berwick Street, Soho.
21. **The Trocadero/Argyll Rooms**, 14-15 Coventry Street, Soho, W1D 7DH.
22. **Museum of Anatomy and Pathology**, 4 Coventry Street, Soho, W1D 6BL
23. **Café de Paris**, 3-4 Coventry Street, Soho, W1D 6BL.
24. **Lyons' Corner House**, 7-14 Coventry Street, Soho, W1D 6DG.
25. **Savile House**, 5-6 Leicester Square, Soho.
26. **Empire Palace of Varieties**, 5-6 Leicester Square, Soho, WC2H 7NA.
27. **Alhambra**, 24-26 Leicester Square, Soho, WC2H 7JY.
28. **Hotel de Provence**, 22 Leicester Square, Soho, WC2H 7LE.
29. **Hippodrome**, Cranbourn Street / Leicester Square, Soho.
30. **Dalton's Club**, Leicester Square, Soho.

Starting at Hyde Park Corner and working eastwards, Apsley House (1), 149 Piccadilly, was once known as 'Number 1, London'. It was the home of the Duke of Wellington, hero of Waterloo, twice Prime Minister, inventor of the boot and, once upon a time, the lover of one of the greatest nineteenth-century courtesans, Harriette Wilson. When she was ageing and fading, she wrote to her former lovers suggesting they pay an annuity rather than appear in her forthcoming memoirs. The Duke is reputed to have told her to 'publish and be damned'. In fact, it is more likely he wrote this in 1824 to John Stockdale, Wilson's publisher. Correct or not, he was rewarded with an unflattering portrait. The Duke was, she wrote, 'most unentertaining . . . very uphill work', and 'in the evenings, when he wore his broad red ribbon, he looked very much like a rat-catcher'.

The fifth assassination attempt on Queen Victoria came on 27 June 1850 when she was being driven through the gates of Cambridge House (2), on the north side overlooking Green Park, where she had been visiting her uncle, the Duke of Cambridge. Most of her other would-be assassins had shot at her but former lieutenant in the 10th Hussars Robert Pate hit her over the head several times with a small black cane. The Queen was left with a black eye and a scar. That night, however, she was well enough to attend the Italian Opera at Covent Garden.

Pate was tried for assault. Although he claimed insanity, he was found guilty and transported to Tasmania for seven years. After his release, he married an heiress, Mary Brown, and, after living for eight years in Hobart, they returned to England where he died in 1895.

Cambridge House later became the Naval and Military Club (3), known as the 'In and Out' because of the signs on the gates. It is said that F. E. Smith, later Lord Birkenhead, who was not a member, used the lavatory whenever he was passing. When the porter, remonstrating with him, said, 'This is not a public lavatory,' Smith replied, 'Isn't it? I always thought it was.' The property has now become privately owned.

The Egyptian Hall (4), built in 1812, stood almost opposite Burlington House (5). At one time an art gallery where Géricault's *Raft of the Medusa* was exhibited, it later became a home-from-home for sideshows and freaks. The Siamese twins Chang and Eng were exhibited there, as were another set of conjoined twins, Millie and Christine McCoy, billed as the 'Two-Headed Nightingale'.

Another act was a 'half-man, half-monkey'. He was exposed by the American impresario Yankee Carter who went into the cage and pulled off the creature's mask to reveal the acrobat Harvey Leech, who also worked as an early 'Human Fly', and took him out for a steak dinner. Leech is said to have died of shame within six months.

In its later life, known as England's Home of Mystery, the Hall became the performing home of Nevil Maskelyne and other magicians. One of them, the French-born illusionist Henri Robin, had earlier presented a soirée of magic at a hall in Frith Street. His great illusion was the simultaneous lighting of 200 candles with a single pistol shot. He later moved to the Egyptian Hall in Piccadilly where his best-known trick was 'The Medium of Inkerman', in which a drum on stage was apparently struck by an unseen spirit, in response to questions from the audience. The Hall was pulled down in 1905 to make way for a block of flats.

Bath House (6) at number 82 Piccadilly was owned from the turn of the nineteenth century by the Wernher family. It was broken into on 11 June 1924 by the great Australian cat-burglar George Enright McCraig, and the equally talented Englishman Ruby Sparkes. The police immediately circulated a list of the stolen jewellery, which had been stashed in cushion covers, and as a result the pieces were unsaleable. It seems a price of £6,500 and no prosecution was negotiated for their return. Bath House was pulled down in 1960.

McCraig, one of a number known as 'The Human Fly', when not in prison often worked as a stuntman and was one of the most brilliant climbers of his time. The year after the Wernher theft, he scaled the face of the Home Office for a bet.

Burlington House derives its name from Richard Boyle, the 1st Earl of Burlington, who bought it in the seventeenth century. It was a much later occupant, Lord George Cavendish, who in the early nineteenth century reputedly became so fed up with people throwing rubbish into his garden that he decided to cover the entire street on the west side. His intention was it should be 'for the gratification of the public and to give employment to industrious females'.

The pedestrian arcade opened under a glazed roof and has always been an upmarket retail location, patrolled by beadles in top hats and frock coats. The original beadles were all former members of Lord George Cavendish's regiment, the 10th Hussars.

The females were not always 'industrious' and, at the

beginning of the twentieth century, many of the rooms on the upper storey were let to prostitutes. Pimps used to sing or whistle to warn prostitutes who were soliciting in the arcade that the police or beadles were about. In turn, the prostitutes would whistle to the pickpockets below to warn them of approaching police. As a result, singing and whistling, along with running and bicycle riding, are banned in the arcade.

Driving a motor car through the arcade – never permitted – has also been prevented with the erection of bollards at each end. Their installation followed a robbery on 27 June 1964 when, horn blaring and headlights on, a Jaguar Mark X was driven up to a jeweller's shop owned by the Goldsmiths' and Silversmiths' Association. Five masked men with sledgehammer, and iron bars smashed the windows and escaped with diamond rings and bracelets worth £50,000.

One man who was caught after a £70,000 raid on a Burlington Arcade jeweller's on 4 December 1990 was John Hilton. Those who worked at the jeweller's were fortunate because Hilton could be described as 'careless' with his use of a gun. In fact, while trying to escape, he fired three shots, one of which grazed the chasing jeweller.

In 1962, he had been involved when a shopkeeper was killed in a raid on a dairy in south London. He received life imprisonment, and a month after his release on licence he shot a diamond dealer, Leo Grunhut, in the back during a robbery and, at the same time, accidentally shot his accomplice, Alan Roberts, who bled to death. He confessed while he was on remand to the Burlington Arcade robbery and, in 2008, received another life sentence, this time with a minimum of twenty-five years.

In 1998, Christopher Daniell told the Old Bailey that he and James Phillips, known as 'The Ayatollah', saw Sir Paul McCartney in the arcade and, after obtaining his autograph, Phillips suggested that Daniell should shoot the singer who would then be 'saved' by Phillips. He believed that Sir Paul might give him a reward of up to a million. The plot never got off the ground, said Daniell, because Sir Paul drove off in his car. In March 1998, Phillips was convicted of organising a slew of jewel robberies and received a twenty-year sentence. Daniell, who had pleaded guilty and turned Queen's evidence, received a much-discounted seven years' imprisonment.

On 11 January 2005, the staff at Hirsh jeweller's were held up at machine-gunpoint when a team stole a £250,000 diamond necklace. The robbers were thought to have been members of an Eastern European crime gang, but there were no subsequent arrests.

The austere Albany (7), built as Melbourne House in the late eighteenth century by Sir William Chambers for the newly created 1st Viscount Melbourne, still stands, and is now a very grand apartment complex. Once a set of bachelor chambers, it was where Lord Byron smuggled in his lover, Lady Caroline Lamb, dressed as a pageboy to overcome the no-women rule.

Two centuries later, Alan Clark, the late Tory MP and diarist, lived in apartment B5, which he described as 'the straitened quarters of an Edwardian bachelor on his uppers'. It was there that he seduced two girls young enough to be his daughters, having seduced their mother in an earlier decade. For a time, her husband, Judge Harkness, roamed around London with a horsewhip looking for Clark. He also hired the now disgraced publicist Max Clifford to present his side of the story. Mark Lawson, writing in the *Independent* in May 1994, thought him ill-advised: 'I fear that the effect of this unusual "family-pack adultery" is to swell Clark's reputation as a stud, while making you, as a kind of triple cuckold, seem even more wretched.'

One of the great pre-Second World War conmen was Michael Corrigan, who was arrested in the Ritz Hotel (8) trying to sell a pension scheme to the Director of Public Prosecutions. In a 1930 trial over a share swindle, he had claimed to be a general in the Mexican Army during the revolution, modestly admitting that anyone who commanded 200 men was automatically a general.

For the 1930 swindle, he served five years and was sentenced to another two years in 1937. Unwilling to face another sentence, he committed suicide, hanging himself in prison with an Old Etonian tie, or so the story goes.

It is said to be Sir James Mathew, an Irish judge who, at the end of the nineteenth century, said that justice in England is open to all 'like the Ritz Hotel'.

In 1825, John Grossett Muirhead of St George's, Hanover Square, met an apprentice outside a print shop in Sackville Street (9), off Piccadilly, where he showed him some indecent prints and books. He also produced two 'skins', as condoms were known, which he bet he could not fit into. One was later produced in evidence in court, and its use had to be explained.

He took the young man to a coffee house where he fondled him, gave him a crown, and arranged for another meeting to have sex. Two other boys to whom he told this story said he had to be careful. The following Sunday, Muirhead took all three boys, one aged fourteen, to an oyster shop, where he showed them more pornography, fondled them and gave them a crown apiece.

Before things could go any further, two officers burst in and arrested him. Muirhead did not deny the events, but he argued that there were no legal grounds for a prosecution: 'First, that it was not an assault, because the prisoner had the consent of the party; and secondly, it was not an offence indictable in the present shape, because it was committed in private.'

The judge took the view that consent did not matter, not only because it was committed in a public coffee room, but 'because it was an attempt to destroy the morals of youthful members of society'. His crime was exacerbated by the fact that Muirhead was a member of the Society for the Suppression of Vice and a Director of the Auxiliary Bible Society of St George's in the Fields.

He pleaded for clemency on the grounds that he was seventy-two years old and infirm, and not likely to survive prison. The judge said he would be treated humanely and sentenced Muirhead to a total of fifteen months. He certainly did survive prison, because less than four years later he was arrested in Dover for a similar offence, and this time fled to the continent.

Parallel with Piccadilly runs Jermyn Street which housed two nightclubs – the Society (10), a haunt of Ronnie Kray, and the 55 (11). It also housed Turkish baths (12), the haunt of hungover jockeys and criminals on the run. It was there that the 'Wickedest Man in the World', the *soi-disant* Beast, the black magician Aleister Crowley, broke one of his specially filed teeth, so ending his practice of biting women on the wrist hard enough to draw blood.

At the Haymarket end of the street in January 1792, Thomas Hardy, a shoemaker at 9 Piccadilly (13), founded the London Corresponding Society, designed to carry out radical reform. In 1794, Hardy and two other members were accused of attempting the assassination of George III with a poisoned dart. The principal witness against them died and they were acquitted. At one time, the Society had over 3,500 members, but it faded away after the Government passed the Treason Act and Seditious Meetings Act.

In 1912, the Criminal Law Amendment Act, designed to stamp out white slavery, gave the police power to arrest on suspicion without a warrant, increase penalties and, at Quarter Sessions, allowed the judge to impose a flogging. As a result, said *The Times,* a number of foreign pimps had fled abroad.

It was at Abingdon House (14), Piccadilly Circus, that Queenie Gerald, who described herself as an actress, fell foul of the Act. When the police raided her establishment, they found a girl dressed as a nurse and three other girls who divided their earnings equally. Queenie, who kept an ill-tempered parrot in her muff, received three months at Quarter Sessions, and when questions were asked in Parliament about how she had received such a lenient sentence, the unspoken answer was that the names in her black book had played their part in matters being suppressed. On her release, she set up at 9 Maddox Street off Regent Street. She later moved to Long Acre and then even further down the social ladder to 86 Newman Street off the Tottenham Court Road.

Lord Nelson's daughter Horatia was born to Emma Lady Hamilton on 30 January 1801 at what was then 23 Piccadilly (15), now renumbered, but near Air Street. She was immediately packed off to 9 Little Titchfield Street, Marylebone, where she was passed off as Emma's god-daughter and Nelson pretended to have adopted her. Horatia married a clergyman and it is uncertain whether she knew of her real parentage when she died at the age of eighty.

It was at the Pigalle restaurant (16) at 196 Piccadilly that 'Mad' Frank Fraser had a homecoming party on his release from slashing Jack Spot; it was where Billy Hill smashed a bottle over the head of a man with whom he was quarrelling; and, in 1961, it was on the pavement across the road in Swallow Street (17) that 'Scotch' Jack Buggy shot wrestler Robert Reeder after an argument there. He had been trying to persuade Shirley Bassey, who was appearing there, to attend a private party and had been ejected by the waiters, encouraged by Reeder. Buggy hit Reeder with a plate and Reeder said, 'Outside.'

Buggy said, 'It's going to be with tools, you know.'

Reeder told him he wouldn't need tools but what he didn't realise was that Buggy had a gun with him. Outside, Reeder knocked him down and Buggy shot him. Fortunately, the bullet went straight through him and Reeder survived. Buggy received a total of nine years.

The Shaftesbury Memorial Fountain of Anteros (18) – 'The God of Selfless Love' – in Piccadilly Circus was sculpted by Alfred Gilbert to represent the philanthropic 7th Earl of Shaftesbury who did so much in the 1830s to improve the working conditions of the poor. Gilbert described Anteros as portraying 'reflective and mature love'. But with prostitutes working from its steps, it rapidly became known as Anteros's brother, Eros.

Between the wars and for a time from 1948, it would be boarded up on Boat Race night, the annual rowing challenge on the Thames between Oxford and Cambridge Universities, to prevent efforts to climb it. The statue was vandalised in 1990 and, after radiography and restoration, was returned in 1994.

In May 2011, Eros had to have a new bow string fitted after it was broken by a Spanish student celebrating Barcelona's victory over Manchester United in the Champions League. He was asked to pay the £6,000 cost of repair.

During the Second World War, black marketeering became a way of life and in this area of London it was conducted outside Rainbow Corner (19), the club for American servicemen that had been opened by the American Red Cross in November 1942 on the corner of Shaftesbury Avenue. From then on, watches, cameras, silk stockings and pens were all on offer in Berwick Street market (20). There was also a big supply of condoms in the club – the US Army did not want their men picking up social diseases from British girls – and the GIs would sell these on as well. The club closed on 9 January 1946.

Coventry Street has always been a provider of entertainment, although not always of the highest quality. The Trocadero (21) site had originally been designed as a Real Tennis court but, in 1842, was converted into the notorious Argyll Subscription Rooms run by the legendary twenty-stone Kate Hamilton. The establishment was closed in 1878 and, four years later, reopened as a music hall.

In 1851, at the height of popular interest in anatomy, 32-year-old Dr Joseph Kahn from Alsace opened his 'Museum of Anatomy and Pathology' (22), first at 315 Oxford Street before moving to 4 Coventry Street:

Open Daily, for Gentlemen Only, from 10 til 10; to which is added, A Series of Lectures, Under the Title of 'Shoals and Quicksands of Youth', as Delivered by Dr Kahn, Every Evening, at a Quarter Past Eight Precisely.

The museum, with over 1,000 exhibits, was intended to show the 'wondrous' structure of the body and to warn of the harmful consequences to health of abuses that 'distort or defile' its 'beautiful structure'. It included some sensational additions, such as the 'head and face of a man who fell victim to the demoralising and destructive habit of onanism'.

Three years later, in 1854, an 'anatomical exhibition' intended for ladies, Madame Caplin's, opened in Marlborough Street, to illustrate 'the evil effects of tight lacing'. Enormously popular among young men and supported by *The Lancet* but rarely showing a profit, over the years Kahn's museum declined into a front for the sale of quack remedies for venereal disease.

In July 1857, it exhibited a Heteradelph, a baby of about six months with a second body from the neck down. Both were apparently growing. It was on view at noon and at 2.00 and 4.00 p.m. The museum later moved to Margaret Street and then Tichborne Street, close to Piccadilly Circus.

In the early 1870s, the Society for the Suppression of

Vice took an interest in the exhibits and, in February 1873, pressured by this evangelical Protestant group, the police confiscated some models from the museum. In December, at Marlborough Street Magistrates' Court in London, the then owners of the museum, Messrs Roumanielle, Davidson and Dennison, pleaded guilty to offences under the Obscene Publications Act and the magistrate, Mr Knox, ordered that their stock be destroyed. The prosecuting solicitor, Mr Collette, representing the Society, asked for the 'privilege' of beginning the destruction himself, which was immediately granted. Accompanied by Police Inspector Harnett and Sergeant Butcher, he happily proceeded to smash with a hammer the first of the anatomical waxes, the fragments of which were then handed back to the defendants. *The Times* thought that the destroyed models 'were of the most elaborate character, and said to cost a considerable sum of money'.

At around 6.00 a.m. on 16 April 1922, a local man collapsed while walking down Coventry Street. He claimed he had been bitten and his blood sucked but, after he was rushed to Charing Cross Hospital, he was found to have been stabbed in the neck with a thin tube. Another man was attacked a few hours later in a similar manner, and a third victim that evening. No one was arrested and there were no more attacks, but an urban legend quickly spread that a vampire was stalking Coventry Street. An embellishment is that Scotland Yard hired a vampire hunter who chased the vampire to Highgate Cemetery where he stabbed it in the heart with a stake, the traditional way of dealing with such creatures.

All was peace and quiet on the street when, in 1924, the Café de Paris (22) first opened its doors. Popular with royalty and high society, the nightclub featured entertainers such as Marlene Dietrich, Noel Coward and the actress Louise Brooks, who brought the Charleston to London. It was bombed on 8 March 1941 when thirty-four people, including bandleader Ken 'Snakehips' Johnson, were killed. The Prime Minister Stanley Baldwin survived the attack and one story is that, with the water supply damaged, champagne was the only liquid available to wash wounds. It reopened in 1948 and was again the regular dining place of royalty.

On 16 November 1950, 'Flash' Jimmy Everett was found outside the premises after chasing a man down Rupert Street and shooting at him. Everett said he had the gun for protection against a certain Charlie Cozens, but his sentence of ten years' preventative detention was thought to have been handed down because in the restaurant at the time was the then Princess Elizabeth eating Dover sole and drinking champagne. On his release, Everett opened a 'villains' club' in Wardour Street.

In 1910, Lyons' Corner House (24) staff ensured there was a special area for the gay community to meet and, in 1925, *John Bull* magazine, morally outraged, railed against 'a well-known teashop and public house in Coventry Street where painted and scented boys congregate every day without molestation of any kind . . . sitting with their vanity bags and their high-heeled shoes, calling themselves by endearing names'.

It was in the Corner House that the Rector of Stiffkey (pronounced Stew-key), the Reverend Harold Davidson, known as the Prostitute's Padre, carried out the reforming work which led to his downfall and ultimate death, appropriately enough in a lion's cage.

After Sunday evening service in his parish in Norfolk, he would take the train to London where, he said, he would try to wean prostitutes away from their lives of sin. He also turned his attention to the waitresses at Lyons' Corner Houses. With their starched dresses and black stockings, since 1924 they had been known as 'Nippys'. That year there had been a competition to devise a name, and among the rejected suggestions were 'Dexterous Doras' and 'Sybil at your Service'. Now, in 1931, two girls made allegations of assault against the Reverend. One withdrew her statement saying she had been plied with port by a journalist, but the second stuck to her guns. Davidson appeared in front of a Consistory Court to show why he should not be defrocked. The Nippy gave her evidence well; Davidson did not. The final straw was a picture of him with a naked girl. He said she was in a swimsuit but it was clear she was not and he changed this to claiming her shawl must have slipped.

The rest of his life was devoted to raising money for appeals against his defrocking. Over the years, he appeared in a coffin filled with ice at Blackpool and finally in Skegness, armed with only a walking stick, in a lion's cage. Viewers were charged 3d entrance, and on 28 July 1937 he seems to have accidentally trodden on the neck of Fred the lion who promptly savaged him to death.

Charles Hirsch's bookshop, Librairie Parisienne, was in Coventry Street. He also published in Paris and translated pornographic works from French into English and vice versa.

Hirsch knew Oscar Wilde and claimed to have sold him various works of erotica, including *The Sins of the Cities of the Plain*. Hirsch recounted how Wilde brought a manuscript to his bookshop in 1890 instructing that it be held until a friend, who would be carrying Wilde's card, came to retrieve it. 'A few days later, one of the young gentlemen I had seen with [Wilde] came to collect the package. He kept it for a while and then brought it back saying in turn, "Would you kindly give this to one of our friends who will come to fetch it in the same person's name?"'

There were three further repetitions of this 'identical ceremony' before the package made its way back to Wilde. Told not to open the package while it was in his care, Hirsch naturally did so and claimed that it was written in several different hands, giving some credence to his supposition that it was authored in 'round robin' style by a small group of Wilde's intimate associates rather than by the Master himself. This was *Teleny, or The Reverse of the Medal*, later published in wrappers in an edition of 200 copies.

It was in Lacey's Bagnio, an inn and bathhouse in Leicester Fields – a precursor of Leicester Square – that Mary Toft, the wife of a clothier and mother of three children, was housed while investigations were going on into her claim that while she had been weeding a field near Godalming, Surrey, she had been raped by a giant rabbit and, as a result, was producing a series of baby rabbits. The date of 23 April 1726 was a significant part of her story, because St George's Day was then known as one on which magic forces were likely to be at work.

Five months after the attack, she complained of stomach

pains and went to see John Howard, a surgeon in Guildford. A month after that, Howard issued a statement that Toft had given birth to five baby rabbits. These births were followed shortly afterwards by the delivery of another seven.

At the time, this was more or less believable. Not long before, a physician had published a tract saying that a woman who stood too long and too near a hot stove during her pregnancy could give birth to rat-like creatures he named 'sooterkins'.

Nathaniel St André, anatomist to the King and surgeon at Westminster Hospital, as well as the secretary to the Prince of Wales, visited her and both saw her deliver two more rabbits. Yet another surgeon was also deceived. Toft was only exposed when Sir Richard Manningham, the King's surgeon, sat up with her all night and ordered her to be kept under surveillance by doctors and nurses. There were no more births.

Discredited and arrested, she made a full confession. Her husband had supplied her with baby rabbits which, while her observers were distracted, she had inserted inside her vagina in time for delivery. She spent four months in the Bridewell before being released without a prosecution in April 1827. Her story caused a temporary loss of income for rabbit catchers as well as a decline in the popularity of rabbit stew, but at least she can lay claim to be the mother of one of the most popular tricks in the magician's repertoire.

Savile House (25) in Leicester Square was at one time a shooting gallery where Edward Oxford practised before his failed attempt to assassinate Queen Victoria in 1840 – the first of the eight failed efforts. He was immediately arrested and charged with attempted murder but the jury acquitted him, declaring him to be 'not guilty by reason of insanity'. He was sentenced to be detained 'until Her Majesty's pleasure be known'. In effect, this was an indefinite sentence, and the origin of the term 'pleasure men'.

Oxford was sent to the State Criminal Lunatic Asylum in Bethlem, Southwark, where he remained as a model patient for the next twenty-four years, learning to play the violin. The doctors reported that he could play draughts and chess better than any other patient. He also learnt French, German and Italian to a degree of fluency, acquired some knowledge of Spanish, Greek and Latin, and was employed as a painter and decorator within the confines of the hospital. When he was transferred to Broadmoor Hospital in 1864, the notes taken on his arrival described him as 'apparently sane'. He still claimed the pistols he had fired at the Queen were not loaded with anything other than powder, and that his attack was fuelled not by a desire to injure her, but purely by a desire for notoriety.

When it was clear to the hospital's governors that he was of sound mind and no longer a threat to society, George Grey, the then Home Secretary, ignored the request to order his release. It was not until three years later that a new Home Secretary offered to discharge Oxford, on the condition that he leave for Australia and, if he ever returned to the United Kingdom, he would be imprisoned for life.

The Queen believed that had Oxford been hanged straight away, it would have acted as a deterrent to the other failed attempts.

At the time, part of Savile House was leased by the needle-worker Mary Linwood who exhibited her needlework copies of paintings by Gainsborough and Reynolds. Originally intended as an opera house, it was also home to conjurors, wrestlers and other entertainers. After Mary's death until 1848, the Linwood Gallery, converted into a theatre and known as the Walhalla, was used by Madame Warton for her *poses plastiques*, which the *Morning Post* described as 'both classical and beautiful'. In 1848, the Walhalla was reopened as the Salle Valentino, where 2,000 dancers could 'enjoy the fashionable Quadrille, the graceful Polka, or the exciting Galop'. By 1852, the Salle Valentino had become the Théâtre des Variétés or Leicester Music Hall, while in other parts of the building there were exhibitions of fencing, wrestling, antique armour, panoramas, clairvoyance and magic.

The building was destroyed by fire on 28 February 1865. It started in the basement, where a workman searching for a leak of gas 'incautiously took a lighted candle with him, and was applying it along the crevices of some wainscoting when a loud explosion took place'. The flames spread so rapidly that very soon nothing but the bare walls remained. The Prince of Wales and the Duke of Sutherland came to see the fire and, after borrowing a fireman's helmet, His Royal Highness 'inspected the conflagration from different points of view'. His Highness, something of a fire enthusiast, was a habitué of blazes and a great favourite with firemen to whom he distributed cigars. After that, the building was reopened as the Empire Palace of Varieties (26), home of the ballet and countless prostitutes.

In 1894, the Empire fell foul of a Mrs Laura Ormiston Chant of the National Vigilance Association. It was warned that unless it cleaned up its act both on and off stage, the Association would object to its licence at the next renewal. On stage there had been an extra high kick by a performer in flesh-coloured tights and two Frenchmen had walked out in disgust. An American had apparently disliked the songs of Albert Chevalier, and, in a sketch, there had been outrageous cross-talk with a pretty young woman saying to the comedian playing a shopwalker, 'I want to see your underwear'. Even worse was what went on in the promenade area at the back of the circle where Laura Chant believed the behaviour was nothing less than open prostitution.

The management did not heed Laura Chant's warning, and the licence was duly withdrawn. It closed, only to reopen a week later when a crowd which included the future Prime Minister Winston Churchill tore down the screen separating the promenade from the bar. He claimed it was there he made his maiden speech, crying out, 'Ladies of the Empire, I stand for Liberty!'

The Alhambra (27), where the Odeon cinema now stands, was another to lose its dancing licence when, in October 1870, the can-can performed by the Parisian Colonna Troupe was deemed too provocative. The theatre was where Jules Léotard, the Man on the Flying Trapeze, swung over the diners in 1861. Léotard is doubly remembered: he created the costume which bears his name.

Over the years, the Alhambra changed its name as well as its clientele. At the end of the nineteenth century, crooks like Freddie Atkins picked up men in the Alhambra and took them back to a hotel room where a partner, in Atkins's case 'Uncle'

James Burton, both of whom featured in the Oscar Wilde trial, burst in. They were never prosecuted.

Throughout the 1890s, hotels in Leicester Square were known for allowing prostitutes to frequent the public rooms, and one of the more notorious, the Hotel de Provence (28) on the corner of Leicester Square, was a home-from-home for American criminals such as 'Chicago' May Sharpe when she was in London on her shoplifting and badger game expeditions. During the First World War it became a favourite of colonial troops on leave and was used by drug dealers, such as the one-legged Willy Johnson, to supply them with cocaine. It was sold to a Welsh businessman in 1919.

In 1900, the Hippodrome (29) on the corner of the Charing Cross Road was opened. The first show featured the then enormously popular Little Tich and, in one of his first roles, Charlie Chaplin. It was also here that one of the all-time great conmen appeared.

Two years earlier, Louis de Rougemont sold the amazing story of his adventures to *Wide World Magazine*. He had apparently been shipwrecked somewhere near the Australian mainland, something only he and the ship's dog, which had valiantly dragged him through the waves, survived. Two years later, two Aborigines arrived on the island and, having together built a boat, they all sailed for the mainland, where he married a local girl called Yamba.

His incredible adventures continued. Alligators were wrestled, emus shot and eaten, and battles fought, with the losing tribesmen being eaten themselves. Later, Yamba ate her child to leave the only available food for Rougemont when he was taken ill. Then he decided to return to England, sadly without the gallant Yamba. His articles were a tour de force and he lectured widely on the strength of them.

When the *Daily Chronicle* challenged Rougemont to prove his story, he could not do so. He was, in fact, the Swiss-born Henri Louis Grien. Aged sixteen, he had run away from home and been taken up by the fading actress Fanny Kemble, who took him on her theatrical tours. All the information for his story had come from the diaries of a man who had left them behind in a Sydney restaurant, supplemented by research at the British Museum.

For a time, Grien became a music-hall turn riding turtles in a 100,000-gallon tank in the well of the Hippodrome, but soon he was reduced to selling matches in Piccadilly. He died aged seventy-four on 10 June 1921.

By October 2005, the building had gone through a number of metamorphoses and was now a nightclub. Indeed, the Hippodrome, which was promoting 'Monday night is Chinese night', fell foul of the Triads in 2002 when warring gangs of the 14K and the WSW (Wo Shin Wo), with up to a hundred youths involved, fought each other. The promotion night was dropped later that year and there were objections to a renewal of the licence for the premises. After a series of conditions were agreed, including the use of security cameras to record the faces of club-goers, it was granted. Two months later, in December 2005, the club closed after rival Triad gangs again fought in and outside the premises. It reopened as a high-end casino in 2012.

Further up the scale were the nightclubs run by the

celebrated Kate Meyrick and her daughters. She was the wife of a Dublin doctor and a stern, rather dumpy little woman. In 1919, she was nursing her daughter May during the influenza epidemic when she answered an advertisement placed by George Dalton Murray: 'Fifty pounds wanted for partnership to run tea dances.' And her career was born.

In April 1919, they set up Dalton's Club (30) in Leicester Square as 'a rendezvous for members of the theatrical and variety professions and their friends'. The friends seem to have been an eclectic mixture. It was the beginning of undercover officers in top hats and white ties and, between 22 September and 5 October that year, according to Sergeant George Goddard who was keeping observation under cover, 292 prostitutes were seen to leave the club. 'I was so cleverly disguised, if I might say so, that my own colleagues failed to recognise me,' he told the court.

Herbert Muskett, the senior partner of the solicitors Wontners, who regularly prosecuted in club cases, thought Dalton's 'an absolute sink of iniquity'. 'We are trying to keep [the actor and drug dealer Lionel] Belcher out and other dope fiends,' Mrs Meyrick plaintively told the police. On 28 January 1920, she and Dalton were each fined £50 with 25 guineas costs.

CHAPTER SEVEN

Covent Garden

Covent Garden derives its name from the garden of the Convent of St Peter of Westminster, a Benedictine abbey. Home until the end of the twentieth century to a fruit and vegetable market, both it and neighbouring Seven Dials, designed in the early 1690s to be the most fashionable address in London, deteriorated sharply during the eighteenth and nineteenth centuries. Far from the place to see and be seen as it is now, the area became little more than a red-light district and home to slum dwellings before its regeneration began in the second half of the last century.

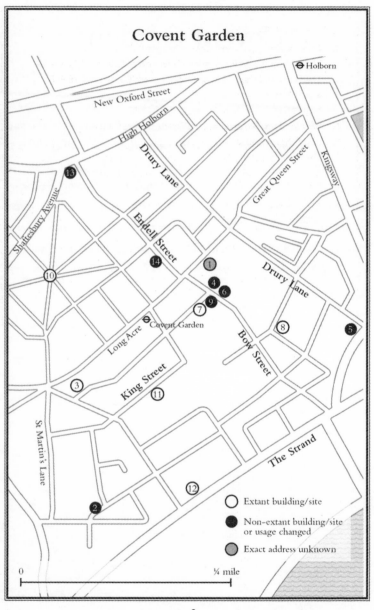

Covent Garden

⊖ Holborn

New Oxford Street

High Holborn

Drury Lane

Great Queen Street

Kingsway

Shaftesbury Avenue

⑬

Endell Street

Drury Lane

⑩

⑭

①

④
⑥

⑦ ⑨

⑧

⑤

❖ Covent Garden

Long Acre

Bow Street

③

King Street

⑪

St. Martin's Lane

The Strand

⑫

❷

◯ Extant building/site

● Non-extant building/site
   or usage changed

◉ Exact address unknown

0   ¼ mile

7. COVENT GARDEN

1. **Cock Tavern**, Bow Street, Covent Garden.
2. **The Hole in the Wall**, Chandos Place, Covent Garden, WC2N 4HS.
3. **The Lamb and Flag**, 33 Rose Street, Covent Garden, WC2E 9EB.
4. **4 Bow Street**, magistrates' court, Covent Garden, WC2E 7AT.
5. **Eagle Hut**, 30 Aldwych, Aldwych, WC2B 4BG.
6. **Bow Street police station**, Bow Street, Covent Garden.
7. **Royal Opera House**, Bow Street, Covent Garden.
8. **Theatre Royal Drury Lane**, Catherine Street, Covent Garden.
9. **Garrick's Head and Town Hotel**, 27 Bow Street, Covent Garden, WC2E.
10. **Seven Dials**, Covent Garden, WC2H 9HD.
11. **William Ewart Gladstone's house**, 10 King Street, Covent Garden, WC2E 8HN.
12. **Stage door of the Adelphi Theatre**, opposite 28 Maiden Lane, Covent Garden, WC2E 7JS.
13. **James Kitten's Café**, Great White Lion Street, Covent Garden.
14. **Caravan Club**, basement of 81 Endell Street, Covent Garden, WC2H 9AJ.

Law books suggest that the first prosecution for obscenity was of Sir Charles Sedley in 1663, but it was not quite like that. The case did, however, set the standard of what was tolerated in the way of public indecency. After a night on the town with his friends Lord Buckhurst and Sir Thomas Ogle, Sedley, a friend of King Charles II, had stripped naked on the balcony of the Cock Tavern (1) in Bow Street and had urinated on the crowd below which, in turn, had pelted him and his friends with bottles they had thrown over the balcony. Other reports have him defecating on the crowd. Sentencing Sedley to a week's imprisonment, a fine and binding him over to be of good behaviour, according to the diarist Samuel Pepys the Lord Chief Justice said that it was because of 'wretches like him that God's anger and judgment hang over us'.

Claude Duval, the dashing French-born highwayman, was finally arrested at the Hole in the Wall (2) in Chandos Place, Covent Garden, in 1670. One story about him is that after holding up a coach, he danced with the man's wife before stealing £100.

Although various titled ladies pleaded for his life, he was hanged at Tyburn on 21 January. His corpse was laid out in the Tangier Tavern, St Giles, and a memorial stone in St Paul's, Covent Garden, reads, 'Here lies Duval: Reader, if male thou art, Look to thy purse; if female, to thy heart'.

According to the lawyer William Ballantine, it was around St Giles that William Burke, the surviving half of the Scottish body-snatchers Burke and Hare, eked out his last days begging in New Oxford Street with a dog and a woman who joined him each evening. He had, it seems, been blinded as a result of being thrown in a lime pit after his release from prison.

In 1679, the poet John Dryden was attacked outside the Lamb and Flag (3) in Rose Street, a dark and narrow alley off Floral Street, possibly at the insistence of the Duchess of Portsmouth, Louise de Keroualle, mistress of Charles II, for allegedly having written some unflattering verses about her. Known by Nell Gwyn as 'Squintabella', she was unpopular in London for being both French and a Catholic. But an alternative and credible culprit may have been John Wilmot, the Earl of Rochester, another of Dryden's targets. Despite Dryden depositing £50 with Child's Bank in Fleet Street as a reward, the guilty party responsible for the attack was never identified. A home for prize-fighting, the pub was also known as the Bucket of Blood.

Number 4 Bow Street, originally built by James Browne at the beginning of the eighteenth century, was used as a magistrates' court (4) from 1740. It was there that Henry Fielding, the author of *Tom Jones*, presided. It was also where he founded the Bow Street Runners, the forerunner of the modern police force. In 1749, he put together six men who would be paid for securing convictions and could take private commissions or rewards. Fielding called them 'thief-takers', and the name 'Bow Street Runners' was not coined until later in the century. They faded away after the founding of the Metropolitan Police in 1829.

Following his death, Fielding was succeeded by his blind half-brother John who sat as a magistrate and wore a black bandage covering his eyes, in front of whom the great adventurer

Casanova appeared on one occasion. Casanova was bound over to be of good behaviour after being accused of assault by a prostitute with whom he had fallen in love – Genevieve de Charpillon – and who had fallen out with him. He took revenge by buying a parrot and teaching it to say, 'Miss Charpillon is more of a whore than her mother.'

Many of the early records of the Bow Street Runners were destroyed in the Gordon Riots of 1780. The riots were, at least in part, an anti-Catholic protest led by Lord George Gordon against the Papists Act 1778, designed to reduce discrimination against British Catholics. The magistrates' court became a target, and records of arrest history and convictions were burned to expunge the rioters' criminal records. Gordon was later arrested and acquitted of high treason.

In 1832, the Metropolitan Police Service built a new station house on the site of numbers 33–34. A new magistrates' court was designed by John Taylor at a cost of £38,400 and was constructed between 1879 and 1881. Oscar Wilde was charged with gross indecency at the court in 1895; following an overnight stay on remand, he ordered tea, toast and eggs from the nearby Tavistock Hotel, which were delivered to his cell.

In 1961, philosopher Bertrand Russell, then aged 89, was brought to the court after demonstrating as part of the Campaign for Nuclear Disarmament. He later spent a week in Brixton Prison. Eight years later, the Kray Twins were committed for trial from Bow Street. The court house closed in July 2006 as its Grade II listing meant it was no longer economically viable to maintain.

In March 1919, Metropolitan Police officers found a group

of American servicemen playing dice outside the Eagle Hut (5), a rest and relaxation centre set up by the YMCA at Aldwych. The club could serve up to 5,000 meals a day and it was calculated that 134,556 meals had been served in the previous month alone. When the servicemen were advised by the police officers that dice playing was illegal, they protested that they had won the Great War for the British and that they would do as they pleased.

When the officers arrested the men, a crowd gathered and a pitched battle began. An American military policeman, Corporal Zimmerman, addressed the crowd, which by now was possibly over 1,000 strong, stating that he would stop the trouble himself. Unfortunately, believing that a Sergeant Wilson standing by him was about to draw a firearm from under his coat, officers knocked Zimmerman down with their truncheons and took him and the other arrested men back to Bow Street.

Later that night, a rumour circulated that Zimmerman had died in police custody and, despite the efforts of YMCA staff and American officers to assure the crowd that this was untrue, demonstrators proceeded to throw bricks and stones at Bow Street Police Station (6). Police officers forced the crowd back with baton charges. Later that night, mounted police cleared the street of servicemen. Thirty servicemen were arrested. The Eagle Hut closed its doors in August of that year. The incident became known as the Battle of Bow Street.

Opposite Bow Street Court is the Royal Opera House (7) where, on a first night of the Italian Opera, one of the great pickpockets of the eighteenth century, the Irish-born George

Barrington, stole a snuff box belonging to Count Gregory Orloff, a great favourite of Catherine the Great. It was said to be worth £30,000, but Orloff refused to prosecute. In 1790, Barrington was transported to Australia for another theft. There he seems to have reformed, because later he became the High Constable of Parramatta, now a suburb of Sydney.

In 1716, there had been an attempt on the life of the future George II at Drury Lane Theatre (8), in which his guard was shot dead when the attacker attempted to get into the royal box. It was an incident which boosted the future king's popularity.

Similarly, on 15 May 1800, there were two attempts on the life of King George III. The first came when shots were fired at the King as he attended a review of the First Foot Guards in Hyde Park. One bullet hit a Navy Office clerk who survived. Then, in the evening, James Hadfield, an ex-Army officer, tried to shoot the King from the orchestra pit as the National Anthem was played before a performance of Colley Cibber's *She Would, and She Would Not* at the same theatre. The King displayed considerable sang-froid, coming to the front of the box and bowing, and, with the audience cheering wildly, 'God Save the King' was sung twice more, once with an *ad hoc* verse written by the playwright Richard Sheridan. Hadfield, who had received severe head wounds in Flanders and who from time to time thought he was the real King George, was adjudged insane and ordered to be detained in Bedlam at His Majesty's pleasure. He died there in January 1841.

It was at the Garrick's Head and Town Hotel (9) in Bow Street that Renton Nicholson opened his Judge and Jury Society in 1842. An inveterate self-publicist, he posed as Chief

Baron Nicholson and, wearing a wig and gown and drinking brandy and smoking a cigar, he presided over mock trials which satirised the divorce suits and criminal cases of the day. The actors often mimicked famous lawyers and men played the parts of women. The audience paid a shilling admission which included a glass of grog and a cigar.

In 1844, Nicholson moved his show to the Coal Hole at 81 Strand, where it remained until 1858, when he moved to the Cider Cellar in Maiden Lane. That year, one of his trials satirised the attention given by the public to prostitution; a transcript was printed and sold well.

Despite his mockery, the judiciary was generally kind to him when he appeared before them, often in debt and bank-ruptcy proceedings. When cross-examined by Sergeant Byles in the case of Bickley v. Tasker, he was asked if he appeared at the Garrick's Head as the Baron of the Exchequer. 'Very barren of the exchequer, sir, I am sorry to say . . .' The Chief Justice Sir John Jervis joined in the laughter, adding that Nicholson was a very old client of his.

Nicholson also introduced the *poses plastiques* at the Garrick Hotel. Young women in scenes from 'Operas and Dramas' posed apparently naked in tableaux such as 'The Sultan's Favourite returning from the Bath'. At one time, women were banned from the audience. Another of Nicholson's enterprises was his refurbishment of the Cremorne Gardens in Victoria.

It was in the summer of 1732 that John Waller, a profes-sional informer and witness, was placed in the pillory at Seven Dials (10). The beadles and constables do not seem to have made any effort to protect the highly disliked man and he was pelted with large stones and bottles before being pulled from the stocks and kicked and beaten to death. A verdict of wilful murder by persons unknown was recorded.

On 19 May 1853, William Ewart Gladstone, then Chancellor of the Exchequer, committed one of the indiscretions that has linked his name to the prostitution of the time. Opinion is divided over whether he saved prostitutes from sin or saved them until later, but that particular evening he met a girl in Long Acre and took her back to his King Street house (11). Unfortunately, he was seen by a young man, William Wilson, who thought that if Gladstone did not want the incident shared with the general public he would have to find him a position at the Inland Revenue. Gladstone, like Wellington in his dealings with Harriette Wilson, was made of sterner stuff. Prosecuted under the Libel Act 1843, Wilson received a year's hard labour, later halved following representations from Gladstone.

At about 7.00 p.m. on 16 December 1897, as he was entering the Adelphi Theatre (12) through the stage door in Maiden Lane to prepare for the evening's performance of *Secret Service*, actor-manager William Terriss was stabbed to death by deranged fellow actor Richard Archer Prince. Over the years, Terriss had helped the younger actor to find work in various productions, but Prince had started drinking heavily and had become mentally unstable. During the run of *The Harbour Lights*, in which Prince had a minor role, he was dismissed. Nevertheless, Terriss still helped Prince through the Actors' Benevolent Fund, and continued to try to find him acting work. By the end of 1897, Prince was destitute and unemployable. Three days before he killed Terriss, he was forcibly ejected from the foyer of the Vaudeville Theatre.

On the day of the murder, Prince asked for money at the Fund's office, but was told that his request could not be considered that day. He hid in a doorway near the Adelphi's stage door and waited for Terriss.

On his arrest, Prince told police, 'I did it for revenge. He had kept me out of employment for ten years, and I had either to die in the street or have my revenge.' At his trial Prince was found guilty but insane, and sent to Broadmoor Criminal Lunatic Asylum, where he died in 1936.

In the 1920s, there was a considerable amount of racism among the right-wing press, and, on 10 April 1926, the principal target of the magazine *John Bull* was James Kitten's Café in Great White Lion Street, Seven Dials (13), known as 'The Black Man's Café'. Headed 'A TERRIBLE NEGRO HAUNT. THE KITTEN AND HIS "MICE": CAFÉ THAT MUST BE CLOSED', the article went on to regale its readers with stories of women who 'have become the degraded creatures solely through continual association with the coloured scoundrels who frequent the establishment'. There had been fights and stabbings and arrests in the café for drug dealing, but 'one of the most sickening sights witnessed every day in this place is the spectacle of white women shamelessly consorting with black men'. It followed this with another more general article: 'DOUBLE DYED DOPE DEMONS: DENS WHERE BRITISH GIRLS CONSORT WITH COLOURED MEN'.

Kitten, who was from Sierra Leone and had been a chef at the Savoy before purchasing the café, took umbrage and so became one in a long line of villains from Darby Sabini through to 'Mad' Frankie Fraser who wrongly decided to take on a newspaper. He sued Odhams Press and, for his sins, the action was heard by Mr Justice Avory, never notedly sympathetic to foreigners. Neither was Kitten helped when the defendants instructed Norman Birkett, one of the top barristers of the day.

The tone of the case was set early during Kitten's evidence when he said that some of the customers brought in their wives, and Avory intervened to say to Birkett, and to much laughter, 'You have not asked if it is the same wife each time.' There was more laughter when he spoke of a Prince Monolulu visiting the café with his wife. Birkett asked, 'He's a racing tipster, isn't he? He's not a prince really.'

Kitten replied, 'Oh, no. That is what we call him.'

Much of the evidence for the defence came from the later disgraced Sergeant George Goddard. The jury had hardly retired before finding against Kitten. He was made bankrupt when he failed to pay the costs awarded against him. When he applied for his discharge, it was refused on the grounds that he was the cause of his own misfortune, by bringing a frivolous action.

In 1934, a sentence of twenty months' hard labour was handed out to a so-called phrenologist, Jack Rudolph Neave, known as 'Iron Foot Jack' because of a shortened leg and the iron frame he wore to support it. His manager, William Reynolds, received twelve. They were running the basement Caravan Club (14) in Endell Street, described by the trial judge as a 'vile den of iniquity that was likely to corrupt, in fact, did corrupt the youth of London'. Following complaints from residents, police had kept watch for some nights, with one officer suffering the indignity of having to dance with another man.

On the night of the raid, it was packed to the rafters with seventy-seven men and twenty-six women, of whom seventy-six were discharged and twenty-seven sent for trial. 'He's got hold of my titties,' said one man. 'Fancy being found in a poof's brothel,' said a Jean Williams. Rather more importantly, the police found a small arsenal of weapons, including a dummy revolver, two air pistols and ammunition, knuckledusters and bludgeons.

Neave remained in Soho. During the 1950s, he was said to have run a derelict restaurant in Greek Street. There was an enormous menu in French, from which everything except *poisson et pommes frites* was deleted. If, by misfortune, any customers wandered in expecting to be served a meal, Neave explained that the chef was ill but the fish, which he himself would cook, was exceptional. He then sent a boy to the local fish and chip shop.

For nearly forty years from 1757, *Harris's List of Covent Garden Ladies*, an annual directory of around 150 prostitutes working in the area, was published giving their physical descriptions and sexual specialities. The first author was possibly Jack Harris, a waiter and pimp. In 1795, with a high-morals wave sweeping London, the then publishers were prosecuted and fined.

What goes around comes around and, in 1962, Fredrick Shaw published a similar directory in which prostitutes paid for inclusion. The House of Lords, upholding his conviction and acting as a custodian of public morality, effectively created a new crime of 'conspiracy to corrupt public morals'. As a result, Shaw went to prison for nine months.

CHAPTER EIGHT

The Strand – Trafalgar Square to Ludgate Circus

Trafalgar Square is named after Nelson's famous naval victory over the French. 'Strand' is a corruption of the old word 'strond', the edge of a river. Ludgate Circus is named after the belief that the pre-Roman King Lud had created the gate that once stood there. Newgate, dating back to Roman times, was one of the seven gates around the City of London.

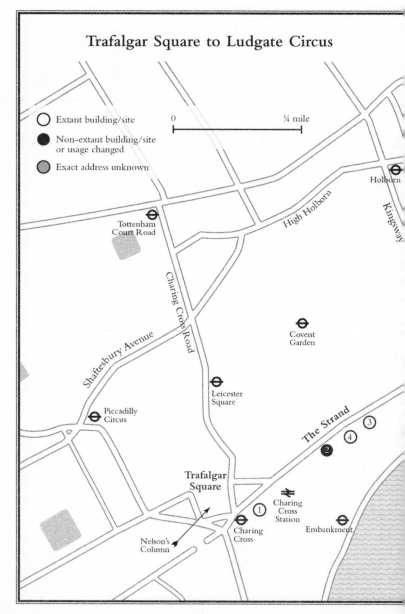

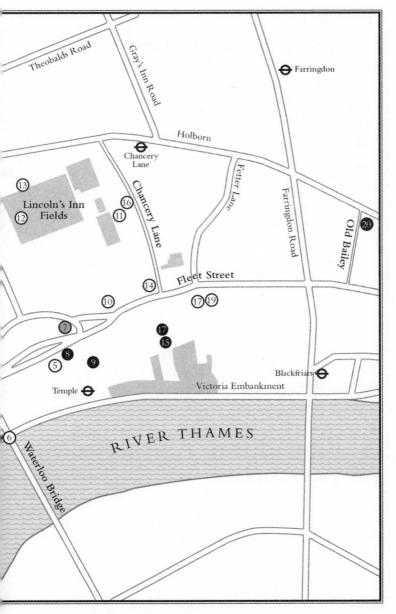

8. THE STRAND – TRAFALGAR SQUARE TO LUDGATE CIRCUS

1. **Charing Cross Station**, Strand, Holborn.
2. **Hotel Cecil**, 80 Strand, Holborn, WC2R 0RL.
3. **The Savoy**, Strand, Holborn, WC2R 0EU.
4. **Savoy Court**, Holborn.
5. **King's College**, Strand, Holborn, WC2R 2LS.
6. **Waterloo Bridge**.
7. **Holywell and Wych Streets**, near Aldwych, Holborn.
8. **Royal Strand Theatre**, 171 Strand, Holborn, WC2R 1EL.
9. **Panton Square**, Arundel Street, Temple.
10. **The Law Courts**, Strand, near Temple Bar, Holborn.
11. **Lincoln's Inn**, behind the Law Courts, Holborn.
12. **Lincoln's Inn Fields**, behind the Law Courts, Holborn.
13. **Sir John Soane's Museum**, 13 Lincoln's Inn Fields, Holborn, WC2A 3BP.
14. **Bell Yard**, Bell Yard, Holborn.
15. **Elm Court**, The Temple, Temple.
16. **Orlebar Turner family home**, 68 Chancery Lane, Holborn.
17. **Mitre Court**, Fleet Street, City.
18. **Tanfield Court**, The Temple, Temple.
19. **The Albion**, 2 New Bridge Street, Ludgate Circus, City, EC4V 6AA.
20. **Newgate Prison**, corner of Newgate Street and Old Bailey, City.

In the days when feeding pigeons was not only allowed but encouraged, Trafalgar Square was home to what was called the 'smutter' game. Controlled by the self-proclaimed post-war 'Boss of Britain's Underworld' Billy Hill, who assigned pitches and sold bags of seed to vendors, tourists would pay a deposit on a photograph of them with the birds on their heads and arms. There was no instant photography and they had to return later for the snap which, along with the photographer, never materialised.

It was a Scottish conman, Arthur Furguson, who is alleged to have sold Nelson's Column to visiting Americans for £6,000 in the 1920s. The story is almost certainly made up as there is no trace of Furguson or any derivation of the name in police records. He is also said to have sold the White House on yearly payments of $100,000. Again, the story is a hoax; in fact, there are no records to show he ever existed. It is possible, however, that someone did. After all, Victor Lustig twice sold the Eiffel Tower for scrap in a matter of months and the New York conman George C. Parker died while serving an eight-year sentence in Sing Sing for selling the Brooklyn Bridge.

In 1990, a demonstration in Trafalgar Square against what was called the 'poll tax' grew out of hand and cars were overturned and set on fire and shop windows were smashed. Nearly 350 people were arrested and 100 were injured, about half of them police officers.

In the days when railway stations had their own left-luggage offices, they were useful places in which to leave trunks stuffed with dismembered bodies, and, on 6 May 1927, one such trunk was deposited at Charing Cross Station (1).

After it remained unclaimed and began to give off a smell, the police were called, and in it was the body of a prostitute, Minnie Bonetti.

A taxi driver came forward to say he had helped a man with a heavy trunk from a block in Rochester Row, Victoria. The only tenant who was not interviewed was an estate agent, John Robinson, who was eventually traced through his wife from whom he was separated. He claimed that after he had picked up Bonetti and taken her to his office, she had wanted more money and attacked him when he refused to pay. Defending himself, she had fallen, hitting her head on a coal scuttle. He left her only to find her dead on his return to his office. He thought she had had a heart attack and, in a panic, he had bought a knife and dismembered her. His story did not appeal to the jury. He was hanged on 12 August that year.

Designed by architects Perry & Reed in a 'Wrenaissance' style, the Hotel Cecil (2) at 80 Strand was the largest in Europe when it opened, with more than 800 rooms. It was owned by the fraudulent financier Jabez Balfour. Instead of advancing money to home buyers, his Liberator Building Society advanced money to property companies to buy properties owned by him at an inflated price. Convicted of fraud in 1895, he was sentenced to fourteen years.

In 1912, the hotel was the venue of the first Eugenics Conference.

On 10 August 1915, the German spy Guy Ries was arrested at the hotel. His case was slightly different from those of the other German spies. The prosecution could not prove that he had actually gathered any material and he was charged with 'doing an act preparatory to collecting information'. Nevertheless, he was shot on 27 October after saying to the officer in charge, 'You are only doing your duty as I have done mine.'

The hotel was one of several which housed visiting Australian conmen who worked a variety of tricks on unsuspecting locals before the First World War. It closed in 1930 and became Shell Mex House.

The other great hotel in the Strand is the Savoy (3), and Savoy Court (4) is the only named street in the United Kingdom where vehicles are required to drive on the right. This is said to date from the days of the hackney carriage when a cab driver would reach his arm out of the driver's door window to open the passenger's door (which opened backwards and had the handle at the front), without having to get out of the cab himself.

The Savoy opened in 1889, and it was there that Oscar Wilde entertained a succession of rent-boys, in room 361. When Wilde appeared on a charge of gross indecency, the magistrate at his committal proceedings said, 'I know nothing about the Savoy, but I must say that, in my view, chicken and salad for two at 16 shillings is very high. I am afraid I shall never supper there myself.'

It was at the hotel on 10 July 1923 that Mme Marguerite Fahmy shot her husband Prince Fahmy Bey during a thunderstorm and was charged with his murder. She was defended by Marshall Hall, one of the most flamboyant and brilliant advocates of his day, on racist lines. Here was a cultured, beautiful Frenchwoman who had been savagely sexually treated by this Egyptian beast. Indeed, it was true that, had she not shot her husband, thus risking a stay in Holloway Prison, she would have been operated on to remove haemorrhoids brought on by his predilection for anal intercourse.

She gave her evidence well. She knew nothing of firearms and it was established that the gun she had used had had a loose trigger. She had only intended to frighten her husband and keep him away from her. Hall, using the florid advocacy of the time, ended his address to the jury saying, 'I want you to open the gates where this Western woman can go out, not into the dark night of the desert but back to her friends who love her . . . back to her child who will be waiting for her with open arms.'

It was one of Hall's greatest triumphs. It was only after her acquittal that it was disclosed that Mme Fahmy had been a teenage prostitute in Bordeaux and had become a high-class courtesan with lesbian tendencies in Paris.

In 2013, the author Andrew Rose wrote that she had, at one time, been the mistress of the Prince of Wales and that evidence which would surely have convicted her was excluded to protect him. She died in Paris in 1971.

In the 1830s, medical schools were in desperate need of bodies for dissection and, in November 1831, the 'resurrection' men John Bishop and Thomas Williams tried to sell the body of a fourteen-year-old boy, said to be Italian Carlo Ferrier, but more probably he was from Lincolnshire. The body was not complete: the child's teeth had been knocked out and, since there was a profitable trade in them, had probably been sold separately for around 12 shillings. Bishop and Williams wanted 12 guineas for the body – at the time a guinea would keep a family for a week – but, when offered only 8 at Guy's Hospital, they took it to King's College (5) in the Strand and offered it to the anatomy demonstrator Richard Partridge. There was a cut on the forehead and Partridge thought the corpse was 'unusually fresh'. After some haggling over the price, the men were told to wait while Partridge changed a £50 note. Instead, he called the police.

Bishop and Williams, who had been stealing and selling bodies at around 9 guineas a time to London's medical schools, had decided killing was easier than digging. They were hanged after admitting a further three murders in addition to that of the boy. The satisfactory outcome of the case from a scientific point of view was the Anatomy Act 1832 which provided that any unclaimed bodies could be used by licensed teachers.

On 7 September 1978, the Bulgarian-born dissident Georgi Markov walked across Waterloo Bridge (6) and, when he reached the Strand, he felt a slight pain on the back of his right thigh. He looked behind him and saw a man picking up an umbrella. The man crossed to the other side of the street and took a taxi.

When he arrived at work at the BBC World Service, Markov noticed a small red pimple had formed at the site of the sting and told at least one of his colleagues about the incident. That evening he developed a fever and was admitted to St James' Hospital in Balham, where he died four days later. The cause of death was poisoning from a ricin-filled pellet. No one was arrested, but it was alleged he had been killed on the orders of the Bulgarian Secret Service.

For many years, Holywell and Wych Streets (7),

approximately where Australia House is today at the Aldwych, were the home of what was then considered pornography. In Victorian times, this included the works of Zola and Balzac, as well as more readable examples such as *Lady Bumtickler's Revels* published in 1872, and the 1894 offering *Raped on the Railway: A True Story of a Lady Who Was Ravished and Then Flagellated on the Scotch Express*, this time published by the pornographer Charles Carrington, who sensibly spent much of his time in Paris. (For those whose lives will not be complete without reading them, and have the nerve to ask, copies can still be found at the British Library.) The publisher Henry Vizetelly was first fined and later imprisoned for three months for publishing Zola even in a bowdlerised translation. The streets were demolished in a grand slum clearance scheme which began in the last years of the nineteenth century and was not completed until after the First World War.

The Strand Theatre, sometimes called the Royal Strand Theatre (8), was on the site of what is now the abandoned Aldwych Tube station. It was there on 28 April 1870 that the transvestites Ernest Boulton, who called himself 'Lady Arthur Clinton', and Frederick Park, articled to a solicitor, were arrested as they left the theatre having seen the appropriately named piece *A Fish out of Water*. The police doctor who examined them found extreme dilation of the orifice in the case of Park and extreme dilation of the posterior in Boulton's case. Their own doctors found no such thing, nor did the prison doctor. The jury took less than an hour to acquit. Lord Arthur Clinton, who had also been indicted, had died of scarlet fever in the meantime. The charge was specifically buggery, and

Lord Chief Justice Cockburn was very much in their favour. Going around dressed as women was, he thought, not evidence. *The Times* thoroughly approved of the verdict but not everyone was convinced, and a little limerick of the time went:

> *There was an old person of Sark*
> *Who buggered a pig in the dark;*
> *The swine in surprise*
> *Murmured, 'God blast your eyes,*
> *Do you take me for Boulton or Park?'*

The lasting outcome of the case was, however, the Criminal Law Amendment Act 1885, devised to protect girls and young women but with a clause added at the last minute by the rogue MP Henry Labouchère making 'an act of gross indecency with another male person' punishable by imprisonment for up to two years. It was this amendment which did for Oscar Wilde.

In 1762, the Ambassador of Morocco had the head of a servant who displeased him sliced off. A crowd attacked the embassy in Panton Square, which later became Arundel Street (9).

In the 1870s, the warren of alleys and rookeries at the Strand end of Fleet Street was cleared so the gothic pile that is the Law Courts (10) could be built. It was opened by Queen Victoria in 1882 to take civil but occasionally criminal cases.

In 1904, one of these was the trial of James Whitaker Wright, tried there by a special jury to lessen prejudice an ordinary jury might have had against the alleged fraudsman.

Whitaker Wright was a man who made, spent and, perhaps unluckily, lost fortunes. He had started his career as an assayer in America and profited by the money to be made from Western Australian goldmines. He ploughed money into building what is now the Bakerloo Tube line and, strapped for cash when his shares in Australian mines collapsed, began to inflate the balance sheets of other companies he owned. He had also ploughed money into his estate at Lea Park near Godalming, creating lakes and hills and an underwater ballroom. At one time, 500 workmen were rushed in to turn a whim into reality.

In 1900 his companies failed, bankrupting investors and members of the London Stock Exchange, but the Attorney General declined to bring charges. It was three years before research by the journalist Arnold White exposed the extent of the fraud, and warrants were issued.

Using a false name, Whitaker Wright fled to America with a young Frenchwoman and was not repatriated until 1904. His barrister, Richard Muir, may have hoped that a Chancery jury would be more sympathetic, but the judge was not, disregarding Wright's explanations that the default would have corrected itself.

The jury returned a guilty verdict inside an hour and, before sentencing, Whitaker Wright pencilled the Roman numeral 'VII' on a note passed to his solicitor, Sir George Lewis. He was correct.

He was allowed a conference before he was taken to prison and, after smoking a cigar and drinking whisky thoughtfully supplied by Sir George, went to the lavatory where he swallowed cyanide. He was also found to have a loaded revolver in his coat pocket.

It seems Muir always thought Whitaker Wright to be innocent, and certainly public opinion immediately turned sharply in his favour. A generous verdict of suicide while of unsound mind was returned at the coroner's court. He appears in H. G. Wells's novel *Tono-Bungay* as George Ponderevo.

Much of Lea Park, now Witley Park, burned down in 1952.

It was from the Law Courts that the safecracker Alfie Hinds escaped while serving his sentence for the Maple store robbery after locking the guards in a lavatory. He ran into Bell Yard across the Strand and down Arundel Street to Temple Tube station. It did him little good. He was caught that night trying to take a flight to Belfast from Bristol Airport.

Behind the Law Courts is Lincoln's Inn (11). When the Old Hall there was rebuilt in 1490 at considerable cost, it was partly financed by fining barristers 6s 8d for 'fornicating with a woman in chambers'. The fine was increased to 20 shillings, 'if he shall have or enjoy her in the garden or Chancery Lane'.

In 1683, Lincoln's Inn Fields (12) was the site of the public beheading of Lord William Russell, son of the first Duke of Bedford, following his implication in the Rye House Plot for the attempted assassination of King Charles II.

The plot itself had been to shoot the King as he passed Rye House, north-east of Hoddesdon in Hertfordshire, on his way back from Newmarket races on 1 April 1683. There was, however, a fire at Newmarket and the races were cancelled. In all, twelve plotters were executed and a further ten imprisoned. Ten more fled abroad and one committed suicide.

Russell's executioner was Jack Ketch, who made such a poor job of it that four axe blows were required before the head was separated from the body; after the first stroke, Russell looked up and said to him, 'You dog, did I give you 10 guineas to use me so inhumanely?' Belatedly, Russell was pardoned.

Ketch, one of the most unpopular hangmen of all time, also bungled the execution of the Duke of Monmouth at Tower Hill on 15 July 1685 when some accounts had him taking between five and eight blows to sever the head.

On Monday, 29 June 1964, publisher and financier Kenneth de Courcy, then serving a sentence of seven years for fraud, escaped by leaping from a window of his solicitors' offices in Lincoln's Inn. He had gone there while his appeal was being heard in the Law Courts. He was arrested two days later, having managed to get as far as the Red Lion Hotel in Fareham, near Portsmouth. A week later, his appeal against his sentence was dismissed.

On 5 February 1984, police staked out Sir John Soane's Museum (13) and, when two men brandishing shotguns burst in, an officer shot Dennis Bergin, killing him and wounding the other man. Four men were arrested outside the museum and a fifth was arrested later. They had been followed from Acton.

It was alleged that the targets had been the museum's Canalettos and a Turner painting entitled *Admiral Van Tromp's Barge at the Entrance of the Texel*. The police had received a tip-off and had been staking out the museum for several days. Amid claims that the whole job had been set up by a police informant, Bergin's brother George received seven years and one Michael Lyons ten.

Sweeney Todd lives on through Stephen Sondheim and Johnny Depp. His barber shop was said to be at 186 Fleet Street and Mrs Lovett's pie shop, where Todd's victims were baked and sold, was in Bell Yard (14), adjacent to the Law Courts. Attempts have been made to establish some sort of historical basis for Sweeney Todd but the supporting evidence is flimsy. One suggestion is that he was hanged in 1802 but there is nothing about any similar case in the Old Bailey papers, in which he would surely have appeared.

In fact, the story of Sweeney Todd seems to have débuted in 1847 in a penny dreadful serial and then in the melodrama *The String of Pearls* by George Dibdin Pitt, which opened at the Britannia Theatre in Hoxton and was billed as 'founded on fact'. It was a huge success and the story quickly spread by word of mouth, soon becoming an urban legend.

Publishers and other authors were quick to jump on the bandwagon. An expanded 730-page version appeared three years later and it was followed by an American plagiarism. In 1865, the French writer Paul Féval moved Sweeney Todd to Paris, and in Australia, Banjo Paterson, who wrote 'Waltzing Matilda', found him in New South Wales.

Lawyers have not often been hanged – in this country at least. Boswell saw one executed for fraud and thought him the bravest man he ever saw. Another was the barrister Thomas Carr, of Elm Court (15) in the Temple, described as both having a fair practice and being a 'low attorney'.

It was a curious affair. On 15 October 1737, Elizabeth Adams, aided by her lover Carr, allegedly robbed William Quarrington of 93 guineas and a diamond ring at the Angel and Crown, Shire Lane, off Fleet Street. Quarrington had gone to the tavern with a girl and, while they were there, the potman suggested he might have been robbed. To show he had not, Quarrington pulled out his purse. The girl was nevertheless thrown out.

Adams and Carr, wearing a 'silver lac'd waistcoat', along with Mrs Prevost the landlady, persuaded Quarrington to stay, saying he might be set upon if he left, and they drank three or four bottles of wine together. At about 2.00 a.m., Quarrington decided to stay the night, and he said he had not been in his room more than a few minutes when Adams, Carr, Mrs Prevost and some others set about him, with Carr holding a knife to his throat. After they had robbed him, they forced him, he said, to drink another couple of bottles of wine. The next morning, unhindered, he left the house and went to report the incident.

Carr maintained he had been in his chambers at the time and the only reason he had ever been in the tavern was because he was defending Mrs Prevost on a charge of keeping a disorderly house. Despite his calling a judge and several barristers to give evidence on his behalf, the jury found both him and Elizabeth guilty.

Although she dutifully attended divine services in prison, Carr did not, saying the pain in his legs made it impossible to climb stairs and that he had other things to do. Not the sort of behaviour to win pardons, and when Carr did ask for Royal Mercy, the Privy Council was extremely sniffy, saying, 'a flagrant breach of the law was greatly aggravated in being committed by a man professing the law'. They were hanged at Tyburn the following January. Mrs Prevost was never charged.

One of the great miscarriages of justice took place with the hanging in July 1815 of eighteen-year-old Elizabeth Fenning, cook to the Orlebar Turner family at 68 Chancery Lane (16). When the entire household, including Elizabeth, were taken ill after dinner, it was decided that, even though she had eaten them herself, because the dumplings were unusually floury she must have poisoned them.

Tried for attempted murder with no clear evidence against her and no one really able to explain the symptoms of arsenical poisoning, she was convicted after a hostile summing up by the Recorder. Efforts to save her from the gallows were unsuccessful, and her funeral at St George the Martyr, Bloomsbury, was attended by up to 10,000 people. The cause of their illnesses had probably been bad meat, but there is a story that one of the Turner sons, Robert, later confessed to being the poisoner while he was dying in the Ipswich workhouse.

Maud Crofts, Carrie Morrison, Mary Pickup and Mary Sykes were the first women to pass their solicitors' examinations in 1922. The story goes that to decide who would be the first woman solicitor admitted to the Rolls, the four rivals good-naturedly ran a race along Chancery Lane. The first to burst through the doors of the Society's Hall was Carrie Morrison. Unfortunately, it may well be just that – a good story.

In the eighteenth century, it was usual for particularly notorious murderers to be hanged as near to the place of their crimes as possible, and, on 7 March 1733, twenty-two-year-old Sarah Malcolm was hanged on temporary gallows in the square opposite Mitre Court (17), Fleet Street, for the murder of Ann Price, whom she killed in a robbery at Tanfield

Court (18), Inner Temple. A coroner's jury had already returned two other verdicts of murder against her, both of which had been committed during robberies.

In the 1970s, The Albion (19) at Ludgate Circus was one of a number of venues where police and criminals or go-betweens could meet to arrange bail, weaken evidence and share the proceeds of crime. In March 1980, Detective Superintendent John Keane, former head of the Serious Crime Squad, and Detective Inspector Bernard Gent fought in the public bar. The quarrel was over a tape recorder Keane suspected Gent was using to record a conversation they were having about a £10,000 bribe to help a friend of Keane's escape a robbery charge. As they fought, the publican's wife told them that if they didn't stop, she would call the police. 'We *are* the police,' replied Gent. Keane later received three years on corruption charges.

The Fleet Prison, off what is now Farringdon Street, opened its gates in the late twelfth century but, by the eighteenth century, had come to be used principally as a debtors' prison. Prisoners had to pay for their board and lodgings, and one of the best income earners were clandestine marriages performed by either a defrocked priest in the prison or someone pretending to be a priest. These marriages were made illegal under the Marriage Act 1753.

The last warden of the prison was the brutal Thomas Bambridge, who illegally put prisoners in irons and the dungeons. He was later himself sent to Newgate. The prison was pulled down in 1846.

A hundred yards or so up Ludgate Hill, Newgate Prison (20)

on the corner of Newgate Street and Old Bailey opened its gates at the end of the twelfth century and closed them at the beginning of the twentieth. In 1780, the prison was a target during the anti-Catholic riots and a number of prisoners were liberated by the mob.

When executions ceased at Tyburn, they were moved to Newgate, and it was there, on Monday, 23 February 1807, that twenty-eight people died when attending the hanging of Elizabeth Godfrey, who had killed Richard Prince, a neighbour of hers, in a brothel in Marylebone. Also on the scaffold that morning were the highwaymen John Holloway and Owen Haggerty, who had been convicted of robbery. It seems that spectators fell over a pieman's basket and the crowd panicked. It was estimated that 40,000 had come to see the executions that morning.

CHAPTER NINE

Looking East – Bloomsbury to Clerkenwell

The name Bloomsbury is derived from 'Blemondisberi' – the bury, or manor, of Blemond, named after the landowner William de Blemond. Holborn may be derived from the Middle English 'hol', for hollow, and 'bourne', for brook, referring to the River Fleet. Clerkenwell took its name from the Clerks' Well in Farringdon Lane. Saffron Hill is where saffron was grown commercially in the nineteenth century.

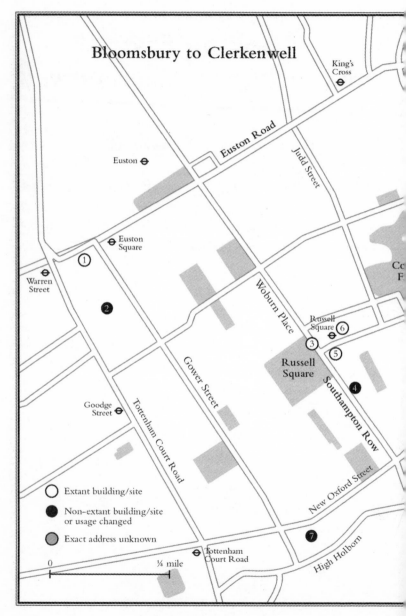

Bloomsbury to Clerkenwell

King's
Cross

Euston Road

Judd Street

Euston

Euston
Square

① ②

Warren
Street

Woburn Place

Russell
Square ⑥

③ ⑤

Russell
Square

Southampton Row

④

Gower Street

Goodge
Street

Tottenham Court Road

New Oxford Street

⑦

○ Extant building/site

● Non-extant building/site
  or usage changed

● Exact address unknown

0   ¼ mile

Tottenham
Court Road

High Holborn

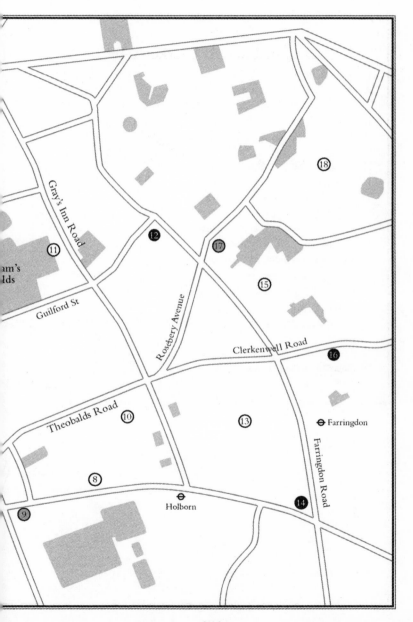

9. LOOKING EAST – BLOOMSBURY TO CLERKENWELL

1. **University College Hospital**, 235 Euston Rd, Bloomsbury, NW1 2BU.
2. **Nursing home**, Alfred Street (now Huntley Street), Bloomsbury.
3. **Russell Hotel**, 8 Russell Square, Bloomsbury, WC1B 5BE.
4. **Chemist**, 134 Southampton Row, Bloomsbury, WC1B 5AF.
5. **Imperial Hotel**, 61-66 Russell Square, Bloomsbury, WC1B 5BB.
6. **Russell Square Underground station**, Bernard St, Bloomsbury, WC1N 1LJ.
7. **Murder of Dorothy Wallis**, corner of High Holborn and New Oxford Street, Holborn.
8. **Hand Court**, High Holborn, Holborn.
9. **Chandler's shop**, New Turnstile, Holborn.
10. **Jockey's Fields**, off Theobold's Road, Holborn.
11. **Mecklenburgh Square**, Bloomsbury.
12. **Coldbath Fields riot**, Mount Pleasant, Clerkenwell.
13. **Hatton Garden theft**, 88-89 Hatton Garden, Holborn, EC1N 8PN.
14. **Mother Margaret Clap's Molly House**, Field Lane, Holborn.
15. **House of Detention**, Bowling Green Lane, Clerkenwell.
16. **Turnmills nightclub**, corner of Turnmill Street and Clerkenwell Road, Clerkenwell.
17. **Fratellanza Club**, Great Bath Street, Clerkenwell.
18. **Shooting of Paul Tiernan**, corner of St John and Wyclif Streets, Clerkenwell.

In 1846, twelve years after its foundation, the first operation with the patient under general anaesthetic was performed at University College Hospital (1) when a leg was removed in thirty seconds.

The hospital itself is said to have two ghosts. The first is Jeremy Bentham, philosopher and law reformer and a leading sponsor of the Anatomy Act 1832 which made more bodies available for medical dissection. His stuffed body is on display in a glass case and he is said to chase staff around the hospital waving his walking stick. The other ghost is Lizzie Church, a trainee nurse at the hospital in the 1890s, who accidentally administered a fatal dose of morphine to her lover who was in hospital at the time. She is said to appear at the bedside of patients who are also due an injection.

The last woman to be hanged in public in London was Catherine Wilson. In February 1862, when she was charged with attempting to murder Sarah Carnell, a woman for whom she was supposed to be caring, the police investigated a number of other poisonings. One of them was a Maria Soames in a nursing home in Alfred Street (2), Bloomsbury. Wilson had persuaded her – and others – to leave her money in her will. She was acquitted of the Carnell case and immediately re-arrested for the Soames murder.

At the end of that trial, Mr Justice Byles commented, 'The result upon my mind is that I have no more doubt that you committed the crime than if I had seen it committed with my own eyes.' Although she never confessed, Wilson was suspected of a number of other poisonings. She was hanged in

Horsemonger Lane in Southwark on 20 October 1862 in front of an estimated 20,000 people.

The Russell Hotel (3) in Russell Square has the dubious distinction of quite innocently twice providing a resting place for murderers. The first was the vain French-born inventor Jean-Pierre Vaquier who, in 1924, poisoned his mistress's husband with strychnine at the Blue Anchor Hotel in Byfleet. They had met in Biarritz and conducted their affair with dictionaries. Vaquier had bought the poison at a chemist's at 134 Southampton Row (4) when staying at the Russell.

The second was Harry Roberts who, in 1966, killed three policemen outside Wandsworth Prison. Before disappearing into Epping Forest, he spent the night at the Russell with a girlfriend.

The nearby Imperial Hotel (5) was involved in a sad action brought by the cricketer and later barrister Sir Learie Constantine. In 1943, he had booked a room for four nights for himself and his family, enquiring first if a Trinidadian would be acceptable, and then paying a deposit. On arrival, he was told because of the views of visiting American servicemen, he could only stay one night. He sued the hotel and won nominal damages.

Around the corner, it was near Russell Square Tube station (6) that, in June 1907, the American 'Chicago May' Sharpe, whose first husband had ridden with the Dalton gang, and her current amour Cubine Smith shot another ex-lover, the safebreaker Eddie Guerin. She claimed it was to pre-empt him throwing vitriol over her, but the more likely cause of the quarrel was over the division of the proceeds of a robbery at the American Express offices in Paris. Smith received twenty years' imprisonment and Sharpe a mere fifteen.

Moving southwards, on 15 August 1949, 35-year-old Dorothy Wallis, known as Daisy, was stabbed to death in her office on the corner of High Holborn and New Oxford Street (7) where she ran a none-too-successful secretarial agency. An Italian-looking man was seen hurrying down an alleyway around the time of the murder. Various suggestions were advanced as a motive: a robbery gone wrong; a jealous lover; a sex attack; and even that she had become involved in the post-war black market. None stood up, and of 300 sets of fingerprints taken in her office, all the owners except one were eliminated, the one remaining set belonging to a person with no criminal convictions.

Then in September 1957, Frank Mitchell 'The Mad Axeman', later killed on behalf of the Kray Twins, wrote from Broadmoor mental hospital confessing to the stabbing. He did have a reputation for office breaking but he did not resemble the man seen in the alley. The general opinion was that Mitchell just wanted to get out of Broadmoor and saw his confession as a means to this end. The case remains open, and there are vague suggestions it might have been a lesbian attack on the basis that, in those days, women usually wore gloves outside their homes, something which would account for a lack of fingerprints.

Solicitor George Waugh was shot dead near his office in Holborn on 16 January 1856. His attacker was a former client, 25-year-old Charles Westron, for whom he had obtained a sub-stantial settlement in a long-running action. Westron was in no way grateful, claiming that Waugh had cheated him by persuading him to share some of the winnings with Westron's family. As a result, he had been forced to live on bread and cheese. He began threatening the solicitor, and things had reached such a pitch that Waugh had taken out a summons at Bow Street for his protection. It had been withdrawn when Westron agreed to instruct another solicitor.

On the day of the killing, Westron waited for Waugh in Hand Court (8), not far from the Old Bailey. When he saw the solicitor approaching, he fired point-blank into Waugh's chest and was immediately detained by the beadles. In March, the death penalty imposed was commuted to penal servitude for life. He was said to be 'predisposed to insanity'.

At one time, Waugh had employed a William Howe as his clerk but later dismissed him. Howe then served a jail sentence for perverting the course of justice and, on his release, sailed to New York where, in the 1880s and 1890s, he was the undoubted king of the criminal bar there.

One of the 1780 anti-Catholic Gordon rioters who destroyed a chandler's shop in New Turnstile (9), leading from High Holborn to Lincoln's Inn Fields, was the public executioner Edward Dennis. He claimed he had merely gone along with the rioters for his own safety and had taken no real part in the destruction. Perhaps because of his unpopularity, he was convicted. He was, however, later reprieved so he could hang other rioters.

On 21 September 1954, in a meticulously planned job, a team organised by Billy Hill robbed a KLM bullion lorry in Jockey's Fields (10), a narrow mews-style street off Theobald's Road, clearing £45,000. The whole operation took less than a minute. The bullion was never recovered and was thought to have been smelted down that night. When questioned by the police, Hill produced the respected Fleet Street journalist Hannen Swaffer as his alibi.

The second Metropolitan policeman to be killed on duty was PC John Long – the first was Joseph Grantham when he tried to break up a fight in Somers Town in June 1830 – who, in the early hours of 16 August 1830, saw three men behaving suspiciously in what is now the Gray's Inn Road. He followed them through Guildford and Doughty Streets into Mecklenburgh Square (11), where he approached them and was stabbed. Another constable heard the commotion and chased and caught William Sapwell, alias John Smith. Housebreaking instruments were found where Long died. Sapwell claimed he had heard a cry of 'Stop, thief', and had chased after four men but had himself been arrested. He was hanged on 20 September.

Robert Culley, the next police officer to die on duty, was killed on 13 May 1833, not far away during the Coldbath Fields riot (12). A meeting had been called by the newly formed National Union of the Working Classes. Marchers carried the French tricolour and the American flag. Leaflets calling for the abolition of the House of Lords and the monarchy were handed out. The police had been warned and marched down Calthorpe Street where fighting broke out.

Despite the efforts of the coroner, the jury returned a verdict of justifiable homicide, partly on the grounds that the Riot Act telling the crowd to disperse had not been read to them. Medals were struck commemorating their decision and they were fêted with a riverboat cruise festooned with a banner: 'In Honour of the Independent & Heroic 17 Jurymen who, in defiance of Tyrannic Dictation, returned an Honest Verdict'. Another man, George Fursey, was charged with the attempted murder of two officers. After he was acquitted, a dinner was given in his honour.

The substantial jewellery district of Hatton Garden has always been at risk of robberies. On 20 November 1954, Alfred Charles Ady and Countess Thelma Madeleine Noad-Johnston, known both as Black Maria and the Black Orchid, along with the American Hubert Clark, robbed the jeweller Abraham Cobden. The trio had gone to his shop which they had previously reconnoitred and chloroformed him. Unfortunately, he recovered quickly enough to see them tipping the contents of the safe and some jewellery into a sack. They rushed out on to the pavement where Clark knocked out a passer-by who tried to stop them. In January 1955, he received three years at the Old Bailey. The day after he was sentenced, Ady and Noad-Johnston died in a suicide pact at the Pack Horse Hotel in Staines.

The biggest theft took place at 88–89 Hatton Garden (13) over Easter weekend in April 2015. The gang, who had planned the raid on safe deposit boxes in the Castle pub and Scotti's Café at Clerkenwell Green, entered through a communal entrance, disconnected the lift and then climbed down the shaft before forcing open the doors and using a heavy-duty drill to bore into the vault. Valuables worth up to £4 million, including gold, diamonds and sapphires, were taken. Two-thirds of the items are still missing.

The gang, described as 'analogue criminals in a digital age', were tracked down due to a series of mistakes, including one of them using his own car during the heist. The combined age of the six men convicted was 448, with the leader, Brian Reader, the oldest at 77. One man only known as 'Basil' is still wanted. Sentences of between six and seven years were handed out.

Further along High Holborn, in February 1726, the police raided Mother Margaret Clap's Molly House next to the Bunch of Grapes in Field Lane (14), which linked Holborn Hill and Saffron Hill. After the raid, three men – Gabriel Lawrence, William Griffin and Thomas Wright – having been found guilty of sodomy, were hanged at Tyburn on 9 May that year.

On 11 July, Margaret Clap herself stood trial at the Old Bailey on a charge of 'keeping a House in which she procured and encouraged Persons to commit Sodomy'. Clap told the jury, 'I hope it will be considered that I am a Woman, and therefore it cannot be thought that I would ever be concerned in such abominable Practices.'

Found guilty, she was sentenced to stand in the pillory in Smithfield, to pay a fine of 20 marks (a measure at the time of weight in gold or silver), and to two years' imprisonment. During her time in the pillory, she was treated so severely by the mob that she fainted and fell off several times. She was carried back to prison having convulsive fits. It is said she died within a week.

A hundred years later, Flora Tristan wrote in her *London Journal*, 'Quite close to Newgate, in a little alley off Holborn Hill called Field Lane, which is too narrow for vehicles to use, there is absolutely nothing to be seen but dealers in second-hand silk handkerchiefs. I am sure I do not need to warn any curious traveller who might be tempted to follow in my footsteps, to leave at home his watch, purse and handkerchief before he ventures into Field Lane, for he may be sure that the gentlemen who frequent the spot are all light-fingered!' Dickens set *Oliver Twist* in Field Lane. The street disappeared with the construction of Holborn Viaduct in the 1860s.

It was at Smithfield Market in July 1797 that a butcher sold his wife for 3 guineas and a crown. He had brought her there in a halter and the purchaser was a hog driver. Initially, *The Times* was appalled: 'Pity it is there is no stop put to such depraved conduct in the lower order of people.'

But the next day, the writer had changed his tune, observing, possibly with his tongue firmly wedged in his cheek, that he had not known the average price of wives: 'The increasing value of the fair sex is esteemed by several eminent writers as a certain criterion of increasing civilisation. Smithfield has, on this ground, strong pretensions to refined improvement, as the price of wives has risen in that market from a half a guinea to three guineas and a half.'

Although the practice was strictly illegal, prosecutions were few and far between and the penalties derisory. At Rutland Quarter Sessions in 1820, the purchaser was fined 1s 6d.

On 13 December 1867, the exercise yard at the House of Detention (15) in Bowling Green Lane, Clerkenwell, was the target of an explosion instigated by members of the Fenian Society in an attempt to aid the escape of Richard Burke, an arms supplier to the Fenians. The blast killed twelve bystanders and wounded 120 in Corporation Row. Some of those responsible were executed, with ringleader Michael Barrett the last person to be publicly hanged outside Newgate Prison. The event became known as the Clerkenwell Outrage.

Originally a warehouse and stables for the Great Northern Railway Company, on the corner of Turnmill Street and Clerkenwell Road, it was outside Turnmills nightclub (16) that the London gangster 'Mad' Frank Fraser was shot in the face. He survived and declined to assist the police, telling them his name was Tutankhamen. The club closed in March 2008 and the building demolished to make way for offices.

One of the post-First World War racecourse gangs was that of the Sabini brothers who preyed on bookmakers, charging them for the erection of pitches on the free courses. Part of this gang were the Cortesi brothers, who thought they should have a larger share of the takings, and, on 19 November 1922, just before midnight, Darby Sabini and his younger brother Harry were trapped in the Fratellanza Club (17) in Great Bath Street, Clerkenwell, by Augustus and Enrico (Harry) Cortesi. Darby was punched and hit with bottles while Harry was shot in the stomach.

Darby suffered an even greater indignity. As he told the magistrates' court, his false teeth were broken as a result of the blows from the bottles. He was also able to confirm his respectability: 'I am a quiet, peaceable man. I never begin a fight. I've only once been attacked. I've never attacked anyone. I do a little bit of work as a commission agent, sometimes for myself and sometimes for someone else. I'm always honest. The last day's work I did was two years ago. I live by my brains.'

He had only once carried a revolver and that was the time he was attacked at Greenford Park. Indeed, he turned out his pockets in confirmation that he was not carrying a gun.

The Cortesi brothers, who lived only five doors from the Fratellanza, were arrested the same night and, at the Old Bailey on 18 January 1923, each received a sentence of three years' penal servitude. A rather sour note on a Home Office file reads, 'It is a pity that the Cortesis were not charged with the murder of the Sabinis.'

The spirit of the Sabinis lives on. In 2016, Patsy Adams was jailed for nine years after shooting Paul Tiernan in the chest as he sat in his car on the corner of St John and Wyclif Streets (18) on 22 December 2013. Charged with attempted murder, Adams pleaded guilty to causing grievous bodily harm.

Adams had been seen on CCTV approaching the car. He had believed that Tiernan was cooperating with the police to set him up. The attempted murder charge was dropped when Tiernan refused to cooperate any further (that is, if he had in the first place).

Index